The Power of the Cross

Larry Stockstill

Bethany World Prayer Center
Baker, Louisiana
www.bethany.com

Copyright © 2006 by Larry Stockstill

The Power of the Cross
by Larry Stockstill

Printed in the United States of America

ISBN 1-60034-353-8

All rights reserved solely by the author. The author guarantees all contents are original and do not infringe upon the legal rights of any other person or work. No part of this book may be reproduced in any form without the permission of the author. The views expressed in this book are not necessarily those of the publisher.

All Scripture quotations, unless otherwise indicated, are taken from the New King James Version. Copyright © 1982 by Thomas Nelson, Inc. Used by permission. All rights reserved.

Scripture quotations noted KJV are from the King James Version.

Scripture quotations marked NIV are taken from the HOLY BIBLE, NEW INTERNATIONAL VERSION. Copyright © 1973, 1978, 1984 by the International Bible Society. Used by permission of Zondervan. All rights reserved.

Scripture quotations marked NLT are taken from the *Holy Bible*, New Living Translation. Copyright © 1996. Used by permission of Tyndale House Publishers, Inc., Wheaton, Illinois 60189. All rights reserved.

www.xulonpress.com

For his tireless effort in lifting up
the cross of Christ,
I dedicate this book to Daniel Ost,
missionary-statesman to Mexico.
His towering crosses over the Faith,
Hope, and Love Centers
drew thousands to Christ.
More than that, he preached, lived,
and died the cross of Christ.
May God grant us all the grace
to focus our total attention
on the One who laid down His life
so that we could lay down our lives
for the brethren.

Contents

Chapter 1 Power over Bondage 9

    God's Day of Liberty 11
    Christ and the Jubilee 13
    Walking in Liberty 16

Chapter 2 Power over Relationships 33

    Overcoming Division Through the Power of
    the Cross 35
    The Bitter Waters of Marah 36
    Healing Relationships Through the Power of
    the Cross 39

Chapter 3 Power over Discouragement 51

    Look and Live! 51
    The Power of Looking at Jesus 58

Chapter 4   Power over Temptation 71

Temptation in the Bible 72
Conquering Temptation Through the Power of
the Cross 76

Chapter 1
Power over Bondage

Freedom is a precious, precious commodity. As Americans we tend to take it for granted, but very little of the world's population enjoys the freedoms and liberties we hold dear. Our freedom is so much a part of the fabric of our lives and history that we sometimes forget the high price we paid as a nation to secure those cherished liberties.

Succeeding generations from the time of the American Revolution to the present have gradually lost that concept of the cost of freedom. In 1775 at Saint John's Church in Richmond, Virginia, Patrick Henry boldly proclaimed his immortal words: "Give me liberty, or give me death." A number of generations after him, the attitude had already degenerated to simply "Give me liberty," until we arrive at our present, self-centered generation characterized by so many who just say "Give me."

Our decline as a nation is unarguable, but despite all our problems and all our flaws, liberty is still the hallmark of America. Each year countless thousands from all corners of the globe still set their course for America, the land of the free and the home of the brave. Our freedom is world-renowned and our generosity well-known. We are unlike

The Power of the Cross

any other nation on the face of this earth—a hodgepodge of people melded into one unique creation called America.

It's hard for most of us in America to envision the world that the majority of the earth's population lives in. Political bondage in so many places keeps men, women, and children under the thumb of cruel despots interested only in creating and maintaining their own realms of power. Others live under repressive governments that dictate the number of children they may have or the religion they're allowed to practice. Still others face ethnic cleansing and racial intolerance on a massive scale. Our American way of life and the freedoms that go with it are a far cry from the reality of their world.

We sit in our nice comfortable homes and don't even think about our freedoms. We can vote for anyone we want to in any election. We can travel freely within our country, and we can live where we choose. We can buy and sell property, a basic liberty denied in some countries. We are free to use our God-given intellects to develop new products to enrich our lives and the lives of others. In short, the American dream is still alive and well.

In this atmosphere of freedom, the Gospel has flourished, because the Gospel is really all about freedom. The two go hand in hand, and that is one reason, I believe, that America has prospered. We have let freedom ring—not just civilly, but also spiritually—and we have embraced the tired, huddled masses of humanity longing to be free. We've held out the torch of freedom and liberty, and God has blessed us.

As wonderful as political freedom is, however, there is another kind of freedom that is even more important: spiritual freedom. When people have the freedom of spirit that only the cross of Jesus Christ can bring, then they are truly free, even when under the control of the most ruthless dictator. Just as our civil liberties were won over two hundred years ago through the blood spilled by the first American patriots, our spiritual liberty was purchased over two thousand years ago through the precious blood shed by the sacrificial Lamb of God upon the cross of Calvary. And just as we must remain forever vigilant to protect our political freedom, so, too, must we remain eternally vigilant to safeguard the spiritual freedom Christ won for us.

In this book, I want to teach you about freedom, not in the political sense of the word, but in the spiritual. God's desire for Israel was to bring them out of the bondage of Egypt so they could live in the Promised Land. That is still His desire for His people today: to set them free that they might revel in the goodness of the land He has promised them. But if His people are ignorant and don't even know what bondages He has already set them free from, then they can never move into the Promised Land of peace and freedom in Christ.

Liberty in the Spirit is knowing what Christ did for you and then having the power to say no to the devil, sin, and temptation. It's not, as some think, simply having the freedom to do whatever you want with no regard for the consequences. That is not true freedom, because when you constantly indulge yourself and concentrate on your "rights," you soon become captive to your carnal desires. It's like a train: A train is only free when it's running on the tracks. If it jumps the tracks and runs through the woods, it's not really "free," even though it is no longer constrained by the tracks. It can go nowhere without the structure of the tracks to guide it. That's how your spiritual life is, too.

God's Day of Liberty

"Proclaim liberty throughout all the land unto all the inhabitants thereof" (Lev. 25:10 KJV). That stirring pronouncement from Scripture is inscribed on the bottom of the Liberty Bell in Philadelphia. The bell was cast in England in 1751 to commemorate the fiftieth anniversary of the colony of

Pennsylvania. When important occasions warranted its use, the bell was rung to summon the citizenry. In 1776, the bell was rung to mark the first public reading of the Declaration of Independence. It continued to be rung at strategic moments in history until its now famous crack rendered that policy impractical.

The Liberty Bell has long stood as a symbol of American freedom. As such, it is respected and revered by all. God, however, has always had His own "Liberty Bell." Leviticus 25:9–11 spells it out for us:

> Then you shall cause the trumpet of the Jubilee to sound on the tenth day of the seventh month; on the Day of Atonement you shall make the trumpet to sound throughout all your land. And you shall consecrate the fiftieth year, and proclaim liberty throughout all the land to all its inhabitants. It shall be a Jubilee for you; and each of you shall return to his possession, and each of you shall return to his family. That fiftieth year shall be a Jubilee to you.

Every fiftieth year, God's people enjoyed a year of jubilee. On the Day of Atonement in that year, the blowing of a trumpet signaled that all the people of Israel were now free to return to their homes and possessions. If you had owed a debt you had not been able to pay, and some member of your family had been taken as payment, in the Year of Jubilee your beloved family member would be set free and allowed to return home to the family. The sounding of the jubilee trumpet marked an end to all bondage, debt, and loss. Past mistakes and debts were wiped out, and a year of new beginnings was ushered in. In that one moment, total restoration was established.

Wouldn't it be wonderful if we had something like that in our culture? What if on the Fourth of July in every fiftieth year, all the debt owed on your mortgage, your car, and your credit cards was simply wiped out? Even more remarkable, what if you could get back everything you had lost during those previous fifty years? What if you could just go back to the home you had lost and regain possession of it? That's unbelievable to us, but it is exactly what God did for His people in the Year of Jubilee.

Only God could have thought of something as wonderful as that. There's never been another culture that allowed people to suddenly, in a moment's time, return to all their possessions and to recover all status they formerly enjoyed. I can just envision it: people running out of their jail cells, long-forgotten relatives returning home, the poor excitedly reclaiming lost property. What a day of rejoicing and jubilee!

Christ and the Jubilee

Christ also announced the Year of Jubilee—not in a political or economic sense, but in spiritual terms. In Luke 4:18, Jesus began quoting from Isaiah 61 as He said, "The Spirit of the Lord is upon Me, because He has anointed Me to preach the gospel to the poor." If you are poor and lacking in this world's resources, Jesus loves you and wants to help you in your situation.

He continued: "He has sent Me to heal the brokenhearted." When your heart is broken and the grief is unbearable, Jesus stands ready to blow the jubilee trumpet.

"To proclaim liberty to the captives" means that even though you may be in bondage to an addiction, depression, or character flaw, Jesus wants to set you free.

"And recovery of sight to the blind" promises that the Lord will remove the blinders of tradition and religion that keep you from clearly seeing His will for you.

Finally, Jesus wrapped up the discourse with "to set at liberty those who are oppressed." Maybe you've been oppressed, wounded, and made bitter by the circumstances of life, but Jesus stands ready to restore everything you've lost.

"To proclaim," Jesus said, "the acceptable year of the Lord" (v. 19). Now Jesus is blowing the jubilee horn and proclaiming, "A new day is here. No longer are you bound by the rules and regulations of the law. No longer does the jubilee come only once every fifty years. From this moment on, the Spirit of the Lord is upon Me, and I pronounce a perpetual year of freedom and jubilee that will never end!"

Jesus has sounded the jubilee trumpet, and because of that, you can go home to everything that is rightfully yours. But first you've got to make up your mind that you've lived in the hog pen and under the bondage of the enemy long enough. You've got to want to hear the trumpet sound that signals the arrival of your Year of Jubilee.

For the Israelites, the Year of Jubilee was ushered in on the Day of Atonement when the priest walked into the Holy of Holies and sprinkled the blood of a bull on the mercy seat. In that way, atonement was made for the sins of the nation. Without the shedding of blood of an innocent animal, atonement was not possible. In the New Testament, however, the blood that marked the perpetual jubilee was not the blood of an animal, but the precious blood of Jesus that flowed from Calvary's cross.

In John 8:28 NLT Jesus said, "When you have lifted up the Son of Man on the cross, then you will realize that I am he and that I do nothing on my own, but I speak what the Father taught me." He continued in verse 32, saying, "And you will know the truth, and the truth will set you free." What truth is He referring to? The truth of the cross! In the thirty-sixth verse of the same chapter in the NKJV, Jesus again refers to liberty by saying, "Therefore if the Son makes you free, you shall be free indeed." Free indeed—what timeless words that speak to hearts everywhere!

Spiritual freedom is just as tangible as are your freedoms as an American citizen. Have you ever actually seen the Constitution of the United States? Unless you have physically traveled to Washington, D.C., and seen it on display, you have never laid eyes on the original document. How, then, do you know what your rights are, if you've never seen the actual Constitution? You weren't there when this document of government was drafted, but when you were in school, a teacher told you, "You are an American citizen. These are your rights." Then she probably read the Bill of Rights, outlining your right to freedom of speech, freedom of press, the right to assembly, and all the other liberties that are so dear to us. As a child, you accepted the teacher's words as true, even though you had never seen the document.

That's the same way you obtain your spiritual freedom. You did not actually see Jesus die on the cross, but by faith you accept that the cross brings liberty from all bondage. The cross is the dividing point of all history—both for individuals and for nations. When Adam and Eve lived in the Garden of Eden, they were literally in paradise. They walked in close communion with God; they had no worries, no addictions, and no cause for bitterness of any kind. After their sin, however, they lost possession of Eden, and the door to paradise was forever closed. They were permanently banished from the Garden and driven into the wilderness to toil all the days of their lives. What an awful, terrible thing to happen, but Adam and Eve's sinful actions crossed a line over which they could never return.

The cross of Jesus Christ represents a "property line." On one side of the cross is paradise: our inheritance as children of God, with all the possessions and blessings that go with it. It is the place where God wants us to live, and it is a restoration of all that Adam and Eve lost. On the other side of the cross, however, is the wilderness of sin we live in if we do not know the Savior. It is a land of loss, pain, and separation.

It's as though there is a fence separating us from what God wants us to have and what we actually possess. We look longingly over the fence at "paradise lost," and we feel our way along the fence, looking for a way to cross over. We yearn for the blessings of health, peace, and joy that are on the other side of the fence, but there is no opening that will allow us to cross over. So there we are—stuck in the wilderness, just like Adam and Eve.

In the wilderness, Adam and Eve had to live by the sweat of their brow; life was hard and relationships were strained. One of their sons even killed the other. That's the difference between paradise and the wilderness. Paradise is full of blessing and abundance; the wilderness offers nothing but cursing and lack. But although the wilderness seems to be separated from paradise by a fence, God has made provision for a supernatural gate in that fence that will allow us to return home to paradise and our rightful inheritance.

That gate, of course, is the cross of Christ. Obtaining freedom, then, becomes easy. It is achieved by returning home to our possessions through the power of the cross. Satan fears our knowledge of this simple truth, because he knows that the cross is the means of regaining all that we have lost. He doesn't want us to ever discover the wonderful, freeing power of the cross, so he does everything he can to obscure its view from us.

Walking in Liberty

Psalm 119:45 NIV says, "I will walk about in freedom, for I have sought out your precepts." Knowing God's commandments is the first step toward spiritual freedom. However, unless you find a way to actually live out those commandments on a daily basis, the knowledge of them won't do you any good. That's why you need the cross. Only by appropriating its power will you be able to walk in God's ways and be free. There are three types of bondage from which the cross will set you free.

Freedom from Spiritual Bondage

The first kind of bondage that you need to be set free from is spiritual bondage. Romans 6:6–7 says, "Knowing this, that our old man was crucified with Him, that the body of sin might be done away with, that we should no longer be slaves of sin. For he who has died has been freed from sin." The "old man" refers to the natural sin nature that resides in all of us. When this part is in control, you will always be a slave to sin, unable to do what your spirit wants to do. You cannot see spiritual bondage, like you can more obvious bondages, such as alcohol consumption or drug addiction; nevertheless, it is just as real. It is a bondage of the heart, and if you can get free in the deepest part of your heart, the outward bondages will often resolve on their own.

Grace in Place of Guilt

The Lord wants to set you totally free from all interior bondages that keep you enslaved to sin. One of the most prevalent inner bondages is guilt, and people have concocted all kinds of way to try to ease their guilty consciences. Much guilt arises simply because, within your own power, you cannot be "good" and do what God wants. Paul addressed this issue quite extensively in the book of Romans. He spent the first three chapters getting everybody lost, the next two chapters getting everybody justified, and the next three chapters getting everybody sanctified! That's how it works. First, you realize your need for God, then you accept His way of salvation, and finally you learn how to become transformed into His image.

Romans 6:7 says that you are not to serve sin but are to recognize that when you die to self, you are then dead to the power of sin. Does that mean you will never sin again once you come to Christ? Of course not! But it does mean that you will no longer serve sin; sin will no longer be your master, jerking your chain and issuing commands that you are powerless to resist.

It's like listening to a radio. If your radio has no off switch, then you have no choice but to sit there and listen to it. You can't turn it off, so it drones on and on. When you get saved, however, it's as though your radio now has an off switch. The "radio" keeps talking and tempting you to sin, but you can reach over at any time and slap it off. Because of the grace of the Holy Spirit living in you, you now have the ability to silence it.

The cross of Christ gives you a way to replace all the guilt of your heart with grace (Rom. 6:14). Jesus Christ was nailed to a wooden cross, and Colossians 1:14 records that He "wiped out the handwriting of requirements that was against us, which was contrary to us. And He has taken it out of the way, having nailed it to the cross." Every sin that you and I ever committed was nailed between the hands of Jesus and the wood of the cross. The spotless sacrifice of the Lamb of God canceled all sin, with all its guilt and condemnation.

All of us have done things that we regret. Some of them are truly horrible things. The devil will always try to bring up all the terrible things you have ever done. But, brothers and sisters, your sins—no matter how awful—were nailed to the cross so that you could go free. All you have to do is walk through the door of the cross and move from guilt to grace. When you do that, you've gone home to your jubilee provision and can live in the land of grace.

Adoption in Place of Rejection

Once the devil realizes he can't keep you bound with guilt and condemnation, he tries another tactic: rejection. He tries to make you think that you're not important to God or anyone else. He does all he can to make you feel awkward and out of place when you approach your heavenly Father. It's similar to what happens when you visit someone else's home. You knock on the door and wait for someone to answer. You don't just open the door and barge in, because you're not part of the family. You wait for someone to answer the door, and then you wait to be invited in. If no invitation comes, you just stand there, awkwardly shifting from foot to foot.

That's how some of you are with God. You can't really believe that you are truly part of His family, so you never feel quite like you have a right to approach Him. You stand out on the doorstep, hoping He'll invite you in, but never realizing that the door is already flung wide open and He is waiting for you to come in and sit down with Him.

Romans 8:15 says, "You did not receive the spirit of bondage again to fear, but you received the Spirit of adoption by whom we cry out, 'Abba, Father.' " You're God's child, and you can call him "Daddy." You're that special to Him. Never listen to the devil's lie that God does not accept you. He embraces you into His family fully, having adopted you as His very own.

Jesus knows and understands the depth of the pain of rejection. When He died on the cross, the sun darkened, and for that moment, He was utterly cut off from the presence of the Father. He cried out in desperation, "My God, My God, why have You forsaken Me?" (Matt. 27:46). He experienced the ultimate rejection, but He did it for you. Because He carried rejection upon Himself on the cross, you don't have to. He felt the pain of total abandonment, so you wouldn't have to. He offers you an invitation today: "Come to the cross. I'm going to change your name from 'rejection' to 'adoption.' Walk right into My presence. You're home now—with Me in My house as My child. This is where you belong."

Righteousness in Place of Religion

The devil tries to use guilt and rejection to keep you sidelined, and they are effective tools that stop many people. However, if those two kinds of bondage don't do the trick, the devil has a third type of spiritual bondage he'll try to impose: religion. That might surprise you, but religious people can load bondage on you just about worse than anyone else. By religion, I'm referring to vain, dutiful acts that look good but are really attempts to win favor by following certain rules and regulations.

When you get saved, you might think, "Wow! Thank God I've been saved by grace and adopted into God's family. I'm His child now, and I'm living in the fullness of the cross." Just about the time you begin to feel good about your new life, the devil whispers in your ear, "Now hold on, honey. You might be God's child, but you're not doing nearly enough. If you were really a good Christian, you would be fasting every week and praying an hour a day. You've got to do more if you want to measure up."

If you don't recognize the voice speaking to you, you'll agree with this religious-sounding thought. "You're right," you think. "I've got to do more to prove my love for God." And so begins the endless treadmill of doing more and more to win God's approval, but never quite feeling like you are doing enough. The joy of your new life in Christ soon evaporates, and your sweet relationship with Jesus becomes a dull drudge full of what you have to do and what you can't do.

It's like Joyce Meyer said: The devil focuses on what you *do,* but God focuses on the *who.* It's who you are in Christ, not what you do. The "who" is always so much more important than the "do."

Paul dealt with this problem in the Galatian church. In Galatians 2:4, he said, "And this occurred because of false brethren secretly brought in (who came in by stealth to spy out our liberty which we have in Christ Jesus, that they might bring us into bondage)." The Galatian church was struggling with those who were trying to replace the liberty that Christ gives with the bondage that comes from trying to follow senseless rules and regulations. Just like then, the devil has all kinds of people out there who can't wait to inform you of all the hoops you need to jump through in order to please God. But when you jump through one hoop, there's always one more hoop you've got to jump through.

That's what empty religion does: it focuses on outward actions rather than inward motivations. The cross, however, destroys the bondage of empty religious tradition and replaces it with true interior righteousness. Jesus knew the fallibility of religion by itself. The religious leaders of His day mocked Him and refused to accept Him. They were too busy following their rules and imposing them on others to recognize the One who walked among them. Knowing their hearts, Jesus refused to play their game, and He doesn't want you bound up in it, either. Jesus would say to you today: "It's not about religion. You don't have to do anything anymore to win My approval. There are no more hoops to jump through. You're forgiven of all your failures and inability to keep the law. Walk through the cross and come into the land of righteousness!"

Freedom from Emotional Bondage

A second group of problems that plagues many people is emotional bondage. People in this group may not have spiritual issues, such as guilt, rejection, or religion, but they are victims of emotions that they have no idea how to control. They go to church and listen to the pastor preach each week, but even as they're driving home, their minds bombard them with all kinds of negative thoughts and feelings. Fear is one of these.

Faith in Place of Fear

Persistent fear is a spirit, and it is not from God. Second Timothy 1:7 says, "God has not given us a spirit of fear, but of power and of love and of a sound mind." Fear that cripples your life is never from God. It is of the devil, and it will keep you in bondage if you let it. I don't care if you're afraid of heights or water or spiders. It doesn't matter if you fear you'll get in a car wreck or contract cancer. Whatever the fear, it is not from God; it is a subtle tool designed by the devil to keep you living in bondage.

I know of people who are afraid of everything, and you probably know some, too. These people cannot leave their homes for fear of what might happen out in the big, bad world. Even in their homes, however, they're still afraid. They think somebody might break in, the roof is going to collapse during a storm, a fire is going to start during the night—and on the list goes. Logic flies out the window when fear is ruling.

You know it's perfectly safe to leave your home and go to Wal-Mart, but to the person obsessed with fear, that is a horribly dangerous risk to take. That kind of fear sounds ridiculous to most of us, but to those who are held tight in its grip, it's a very real, paralyzing force that dictates their actions. We had a woman like that in our church. She was terrified of leaving her home and had not gotten in a car and gone anywhere for ten years. Nevertheless, somehow, someone got her to go on an Encounter Retreat. There she was gloriously set free from this fear that had controlled her, and on the Monday after the retreat, she actually went to Wal-Mart with one of the pastors' wives. The trip was only five miles there and five miles back home, but to that woman, it was as though she had gone to the moon and back. She racked up a big victory that day. Jesus wants you to know that He knows how you feel. Look how Hebrews 2:14–15 NLT says it:

> Because God's children are human beings—made of flesh and blood—Jesus also became flesh and blood by being born in human form. For only as a human being could he die, and only by dying could he break the power of the Devil, who had the power of death. Only in this way could he deliver those who have lived all their lives as slaves to the fear of dying.

Jesus delivered you from the fear of dying and from every other fear. His death on the cross paid that price and shattered the hold of the devil in your life. When you accept that fact by faith, fear is banished and you begin living a faith-filled life of trust in God. Through the power of the cross, faith replaces fear.

Hope in Place of Depression

Another emotion that many people struggle with is depression. I might not be able to prove it, but I think the devil must be depressed! Who wouldn't be, with a personal prophecy like he got in Revelation 21? He knows his future entails a lake of eternal fire. I'll bet the devil is nervous and worried all the time. He can't rid himself of the sound of Jesus' feet when He marched into hell and snatched the keys of hell and death from him. In my mind, I picture the devil as a depressed, worried creature that jumps and jerks at every little thing that moves.

The devil wants you to be just as depressed as he is. He wants you to wrap yourself in a spirit of depression and hold it close. He wants doom, gloom, and darkness to be your constant companions. He hopes you'll get so depressed that you'll decide to just end it all. That's how evil his intentions are.

So many people are embracing this spirit of depression, and suicide is running rampant as a result. Depression is a heaviness of spirit; that's the way it is described in Isaiah 61:3. It's an apt description because a depressed person acts as though the weight of the world is on his shoulders and he is burdened with a heavy load that he cannot bear. Verse 3 of Isaiah 61 also says what the Lord wants to give in place of depression, and that is "the garment of praise for the spirit of heaviness."

Regardless of how you feel about your life, there is hope for you. Jesus purchased that for you on the cross two thousand years ago. It doesn't matter how dark and despairing your circumstances seem right now. Jesus is waiting, holding out that garment of praise for you to wrap yourself in. When you receive it from Him and put it on, heaviness of heart flees and hope for the future enters. That's the power of the cross!

Love in Place of Bitterness

The devil's got one more trick in his bag to try to keep people in emotional bondage, and that's bitterness. It's like he's saying, "I know what I'll do. I'll stir up some person in their family or neighborhood or workplace to say something really mean and nasty to them. Then I'll get them all riled up and angry, and I'll give them all kinds of ideas of how they can get revenge. At night when they're lying upon their bed, I'll paint enticing pictures in their mind of how they can get back at that person. I'll show them how to send e-mails and letters to destroy the person's character. I'll teach them how to give the dirtiest look imaginable. I'll consume them with bitterness until it destroys them from the inside out."

When Jesus hung on the cross, He was offered a sponge full of sour wine mixed with gall (Matt. 27:34). It had an awful, bitter taste, and Jesus was forced to take it. So you see, Jesus tasted bitterness for you. That's really what bitterness is: a bad taste in your mouth from something somebody did to you. When you visit the cross, however, you realize that Jesus already took that bitterness for you. If you will release it and envision Jesus "tasting" it for you, you'll be able to say like He did, "Father, forgive them, for they do not know what they do" (Luke 23:34). When you forgive, you let go of bitterness and move into the land of love. Forgiveness does that for you.

I refuse to let the devil keep me in bondage to some action someone did in the past. So what if the boss gave someone else the promotion? So what if your parents weren't the best parents in the world? So what if your spouse doesn't live up to your expectations? *So what?* You don't have to live stuck in that bitterness; you can let go of it and begin living a life of love for God and others. The choice is yours.

Freedom from Physical Bondage

The third area in which Satan tries to attack is the physical arena. This encompasses a broad spectrum of problems. Galatians 5:19–21 lists some of these. Verse 21 in particular refers to "drunkenness, revelries, and the like," and I believe this is referring to those things that we commonly refer to as addictions.

Joy in Place of Addiction

The devil is the taskmaster of addictions. There is nothing he loves more than to get you dependent on something other than the Lord Jesus. Your addiction could be to tobacco, alcohol, or any one of a myriad of drugs—legal or illegal. It could be to an activity, such as gambling or pornography. Whatever it is, it controls you, and you are in total bondage to the thing. It's like you're nothing more than a puppet, with someone pulling the strings that dictate your movements.

The devil loves it when you are in such bondage that you physically require a fix every few hours. He delights if he can drive you to steal—or even kill—to get the money you need to support your habit. His plan is to destroy you and take you to hell with him. He offers the lure of happiness and escape through the addiction, but of course, it never delivers. That's because there's no joy in your life when you're battling an addiction. Some sadness or inner struggle led you down the path of the addiction to begin with, but you soon find that the addiction cannot fill the void. It only makes it much, much worse.

When Jesus hung on the cross, a spear was thrust into His lovely side, and out from the Savior poured a mixture of blood and water (John 19:34). That life-giving flow from Jesus represents the living water He offers to all who will come to Him. There is no true joy apart from Him, and when He suffered on that lonely tree, He took all the pain and misery that rob people of joy and drive them to addictions and bore them upon Himself. Because He did that, you can bring any addiction to the cross and have the blood of Jesus wash you clean from the degradation and despair of it and replace it with joy unspeakable and full of glory. You can move from the land of addiction to the land of joy, simply by accepting Jesus' sacrifice on the cross.

Long-Suffering in Place of Anger

Anger is another bondage that the devil delights in inflicting upon people. Although it is an emotional response, it affects the physical body. You've seen how ugly anger is—people screaming and hollering, red in the face and their jugular vein popping out. Their eyes are bulging and spit is flying! Sometimes their rage gets so out of control that they physically hurt others. It's an awful sight to see someone ranting and raving, but that's what uncontrolled anger does to you.

The Power of the Cross

Have you ever noticed how angry people can become when they're driving? Maybe they think it's a safe release for pent-up emotions, but they can explode over the most trivial thing. That applies to some of you reading this book. You go to church looking all nice and proper, but the minute the service ends, you hop in your car and try to beat everyone else out of the parking lot. Then you get on the interstate, and some woman cuts right in front of you. You can't believe it—how dare she! Then she adds insult to injury and slows down. Now you're tailgating her in the left lane, laying on your horn and flashing your lights to let her know she'd better move over *now!* You accomplish your purpose as the woman moves over into the right lane. You pull up beside her, ready to glare at her and shake your fist, and just as you look into her window, whom do you see but your pastor's sweet little wife! The anger sort of drains right out of you as you smile weakly and offer a limp wave.

Of course, that's just a humorous exaggeration, but the point is, anger can get such a grip on you that you do and say things that are really out of character for you and that you end up regretting. When anger is a regular part of your life, your body is in a constant state of physical stress, and over the years, it takes its toll. You keep telling yourself that you're going to calm down and not let things bother you so much, but before you know it, there you go again—flying off the handle and carrying on in a most embarrassing manner.

Jesus had every right, in the natural, to be angry. He endured the hostility of the Pharisees and the fickleness of the crowds. He was betrayed in the cruelest of fashion by one He loved. His trusted friends deserted Him, and belligerent soldiers spit upon Him and mocked Him. If ever anyone had the right to be angry, it was Jesus. But that was not His way. The long-suffering Savior laid down His anger and refused to hate. He chose to forgive, rather than assert His rights, and He did it willingly for you and for me. By refusing anger, He conquered it. Facing the cruel torture of the cross, He patiently endured for the sake of all humanity. Because He paid that price, you don't have to. You can bring that bondage of anger and nail it to the cross. You can receive Jesus' victory over anger as your victory over anger. You can live in freedom at the foot of the cross.

Self-Control in Place of Sexual Sin

Our culture is saturated with sexual content. From TV to the movies to advertisements—everywhere you look—sex seems to be the dominant theme. Young people think nothing of sacrificing their sexual purity before marriage, and even some married couples shamelessly break their vows of fidelity. Once you start down the road of sexual promiscuity and compromise, you find it more and more difficult to get back on the right path, even when you want to. That's because sexual needs gratified outside of godly standards of purity and righteousness become bondage. The pleasure of the moment is soon lost in the torment of the soul for the lascivious lifestyle that results.

The Internet, as wonderful as it can be, has become a source of sexual addiction for many men, even Christian ones. With one click and in the privacy of their own homes, they can access the vilest, most perverse sexual scenes from any number of pornographic Web sites. Men are sexually aroused through the sense of sight, and if they yield to profane, pornographic images, they can become addicted to them, just as surely as the drug addict becomes addicted to his drugs.

Rejection leads many people to illicit sexual behavior. Looking for the love and acceptance that they never got from a parent or spouse, they begin dabbling in inappropriate ways of trying to feel close. They open the door a crack, and before you know it, they have flung that door wide open and are involved in the most shameful things imaginable. It doesn't matter if it's pornography, fornication, adultery, or homosexuality—any sexual expression outside the confines of God-given marriage and righteous standards will lead to bondage.

Jesus never rejected those caught in the snare of illicit sexual behavior. Remember the woman accused of adultery who was cast before Jesus' feet? According to Jewish law, she deserved to be stoned, but Jesus, refusing to condemn her, challenged anyone who was without sin to throw the first stone. One by one the crowd slipped away, and Jesus, looking at the woman, said, "Neither do I condemn you; go and sin no more" (John 8:11).

If you are struggling with any kind of sexual bondage, Jesus waits to receive you and deliver you from its hold. The power for that kind of freedom lies in the cross. When you come to the cross, Jesus forgives you completely of every kind of sexual sin and begins working in you to give you the power to walk out of that bondage and into the land of self-respect and self-control.

Blessing in Place of Poverty

Poverty is a curse from the devil. I'm not saying that God wants you to have every little thing your selfish heart desires. His emphasis is never on material things for the sake of having more and more to hoard. On the other hand, neither does He want you continually in lack, never having enough to pay your own bills much less bless anyone else. He desires for you to be blessed financially so that all your needs are met and you have enough to help others.

Galatians 3:13 says, "Christ has redeemed us from the curse of the law, having become a curse for us (for it is written, 'Cursed is everyone who hangs on a tree')." Verse 14 says why He bore this curse for us: "that the blessing of Abraham might come upon the Gentiles in Christ Jesus, that we might receive the promise of the Spirit through faith."

Jesus bore the pain and shame of the cross to break the power of the curse from your life, and poverty is part of that curse.

Look at Jesus on the cross and you'll see that He died naked, stripped of His clothing and every material possession. He literally had nothing to His name, and there He was, the King of Kings and Lord of Lords who left the riches of heaven for us. Second Corinthians 8:9 says it like this: "For you know the grace of our Lord Jesus Christ, that though He was rich, yet for your sakes He became poor, that you through His poverty might become rich." He doesn't want you poor, broke, and scraping the bottom of the barrel every day of your life. He doesn't want you homeless, hopeless, and destitute. He has already borne poverty and lack for you on that awful cross. It's yours if you want it.

Healing in Place of Disease

The human body is a remarkable creation of God. We usually give it very little thought, as long as it is working the way it is supposed to. When something does goes wrong in the body, all of a sudden our attention becomes totally focused upon it, particularly if pain is involved.

God never intended for sickness and infirmity to be the norm. Acts 10:38 says, "God anointed Jesus of Nazareth with the Holy Spirit and with power, who went about doing good and healing all who were oppressed by the devil, for God was with Him." Jesus didn't like sickness; in fact, He healed *all* who were oppressed by it.

Sickness can become a bondage. We get so used to our doctor visits, surgeries, and pills that we almost don't know how to live without them. More and more of us are taking more and more pills to treat every condition imaginable. Then we have to keep track of all those pills we are taking: which ones to take at what time, which ones can't be mixed with the others, which ones must be taken with food, and on and on.

That is not what God wants for his children. I'm not against using doctors and medicine; I'm just saying there is a limit to their effectiveness, and we can't go putting all our hope and trust in them to do what only God can do. Only God can heal; doctors and medicine facilitate the healing that comes from Him.

Before His crucifixion, Jesus was mercilessly lashed. He took those horrible stripes upon His back to pay the price for our physical healing. Isaiah 53:5 says, "But He was wounded for our transgressions, He was bruised for our iniquities; the chastisement for our peace was upon Him, and by His stripes we are healed." Healed—what a wonderful word for the cancer patient who has been given up to die, the young woman who's been told she'll never have a child, or the man who's been told he has an incurable disease that he'll just have to learn to live with! Healing for them and for you is found in the cross. The price has been paid. It can be yours when you take its power as your own.

The cross of Christ speaks of freedom more than it does anything else. There was the Lamb of God, held captive by the nails in His hands and feet. Because of His sacrificial act of immeasurable love, we can forever go free. No longer are we bound by guilt, rejection, and religion. No more can fear, depression, and bitterness rob us of the joy of living. Before the mighty power of the cross, all addictions, anger, sexual sin, poverty, and disease must yield.

The cross is a door. When we open it, we step into a land of freedom, hope, and promise. We close it on a world of bondage, despair, and futility. The risen Jesus stands at that door and knocks, inviting you to open it and cross into the land of freedom. Won't you answer His call?

Chapter 2
Power over Relationships

The indwelling power that resides in the cross of Christ cannot be comprehended by human minds. It's too big, too significant, too overwhelming to be grasped by our finite intellects. When its power is appropriated, however, it can shatter any bondage known to humanity, and when its authority is recognized, it can mend any broken relationship. But all that is dependent upon our understanding and applying its awesome power in our lives.

In American culture, unfortunately, the image of a cross has become commonplace and mundane. It's been used in so many different ways that it has lost its meaning. Some people see the cross as a piece of jewelry to wear around their necks or to dangle from their ears. Others see it as a decorative item to place on the wall in their home. Many more expect to see it perched atop church buildings or prominently displayed in the sanctuary, but few give it more than a passing thought. That's a far cry from the way it was in the beginning when the cross had significant meaning.

The cross was not a topic of polite conversation in the days of the Greeks and Romans. Crucifixion was such a ghastly thing that no Roman citizen could be legally put to death in that way. Death on a cross was a shameful, degrading practice reserved for the worst of criminals; it was not something anyone wanted to sit around talking about. It would be like your sitting around the dinner table with company present and talking about the electric chair. That's just not the topic you would want to bring up. But the cross *is* something we need to talk about and understand. As awful as it is to think of Jesus dying that way for us, we've got to talk about it and understand why He submitted Himself to such a horrible death.

In 1 Corinthians 1, Paul speaks about the cross of Christ and its power. In verse 17 NIV, he says, "For Christ did not send me to baptize, but to preach the gospel—not with words of human wisdom, lest the cross of Christ be emptied of its power." In a lot of church circles today, the cross has been absolutely stripped of its power. It's not referred to much in the services, and it's considered dull, boring, and outdated. These kinds of places move on to "deeper" teachings, blinded to the true meaning of the cross. It's as Paul explained in verse 18 NIV: "For the message of the cross is foolishness to those who are perishing, but to us who are being saved it is the power of God."

The cross is now empty of Christ's body, but still full of Christ's power. Whatever problem you're facing, the cross represents God's power to change your situation. It is absolutely the most powerful weapon in existence. When you understand that—when you get a revelation of the cross—it revolutionizes everything, and the cross becomes the focal point of your entire life.

Knowing the vital importance of the cross, Paul said in 1 Corinthians 2:2, "For I determined not to know anything among you except Jesus Christ and Him crucified." He steadfastly refused to veer from the simple message of what took place on that humble tree on Calvary. That's how I want to be.

It really doesn't matter if your problem is a financial one or a physical one. It doesn't matter if your problem is in your marriage or with your children. Regardless of the problem that faces you, God can work a miracle in that situation when you get a revelation of the cross.

Overcoming Division Through the Power of the Cross

In 1 Corinthians 1, Paul addressed the issue of division within the Corinthian church. Speaking in verse 10, he said, "Now I plead with you, brethren, by the name of our Lord Jesus Christ, that you all speak the same thing, and that there be no divisions among you, but that you be perfectly joined together in the same mind and in the same judgment." The Corinthian congregation had divided into little factions, each represented by a particular spiritual figure (Paul, Peter, and Apollos). As a result, they saw themselves as belonging to different groups within the church instead of seeing themselves as one in the body of Christ. Some were saying they were of Paul, while others aligned themselves with Peter or Apollos. Paul quickly squelched such divisiveness, saying, "Is Christ divided? Was Paul crucified for you? Or were you baptized in the name of Paul?" (v. 13).

Anytime there is division in a church, community, or family, it's because one person is being elevated over another. When church members declare "I am of Paul" or "I'm of Apollos," they are glorifying the messenger rather than the message. The particular church you go to is not nearly as important as the One you're going to church for. I don't want anyone to exalt me or any other pastor on the staff of our church. Bethany members belong to the Lord—not to Larry Stockstill.

Satan is a master at pitting one person against another, and he has been doing it since the beginning of time. He actually separated a third of the angels in heaven from the throne of God. From the time Adam and Eve were created, he worked tirelessly to sever them from God, and he ultimately succeeded. Even after Adam and Eve left the Garden, the devil continued his evil work and divided their family, inciting Cain to kill Abel. Ever since, division and strife have continued running rampant throughout world history, with nations and peoples constantly warring and killing one another.

Division is a sad fact of life for fallen man. Republicans and Democrats square off against one another, and men and women challenge one another in so many areas. Racial tensions persist, denominational squabbles endure, and family problems abound. Division, in all its ugly forms, is the No. 1 weapon in Satan's arsenal of destruction.

The cross is the only thing that can obliterate division. It doesn't matter what kind of division you're struggling with or how deep it is. It doesn't matter how long it's been going on or how firmly it is entrenched in your mind. The power of the cross can literally pulverize the wall of division standing between you and someone else, and it can take the most awful bitterness in your life and make it sweet.

The Bitter Waters of Marah

In Exodus 15:22–25, we find a prime example of how God takes bitter things and makes them sweet. There are a number of observations we can glean from this account. Look first at verses 22–24 NIV:

> So Moses brought Israel from the Red Sea; then they went out into the Wilderness of Shur. And they went three days in the wilderness and found no water. Now when they came to Marah, they could not drink the waters of Marah, for they were bitter. Therefore the name of it was

called Marah. And the people complained against Moses, saying, "What shall we drink?"

At this point, it had been only three days since the Israelites had experienced the miracle of the parting of the Red Sea. Just three days earlier they'd been jumping and shouting and praising God for all they were worth. When God delivered them from the hands of Pharaoh in such a miraculous manner, there was no end to the rejoicing, and I'm sure they all thought that everything would be smooth sailing from that point on. Then, much to their surprise, they ran into a bump in the road and immediately forgot about what God had just done for them. Instead, they began to whine and complain: "What shall we drink?" they moaned.

You probably think that's pretty amazing—that they could so quickly forget the marvelous works of God. Stop just a minute and think about it. Are we really any different? We all love to shout and praise God when we're sitting in our padded pew and the air-conditioning is working just right. But the minute we go outside and see that someone has blocked us into our parking space, it's a different tune. We furiously scribble down the license plate number and run back into the church to find someone to announce that the owner of the vehicle with that number should come move his car—right now! That's how we humans are, and that's how the Israelites were.

There they were, traveling in the wilderness with Moses and needing water. All of a sudden, one of them probably spotted what looked like an oasis in the barren landscape. I can imagine them running at full speed to reach the stream and then flopping on their bellies to take a nice, long drink. To their disgust, the water was not potable. They probably spit it out and then whirled around looking for Moses. The NLT says in verse 24 that "the people turned against Moses. 'What are we going to drink?' they demanded."

Moses, they thought, had let them down. Things were not turning out the way they had expected, and they were disappointed. So they looked for someone to blame. That happens to many of us in our relationships. A spouse, child, parent, friend, pastor, or employer disappoints us in some way, and we are tempted to grow bitter. We don't want to admit that disappointment and lost expectations are just a part of life; it's easier to find someone to blame for all our problems. The reality of life, however, is that any human relationship can let us down because we are all imperfect beings. There is no perfect marriage, no perfect child, and no perfect church. They simply don't exist, but if you think you have a "right" to those things, you'll be constantly disappointed when things don't go the way you think they should.

So there were the Israelites, blaming Moses for the bitter waters of Marah. Moses' reaction is recorded in verse 25: "So he cried out to the Lord, and the Lord showed him a tree. When he cast it into the waters, the waters were made sweet." The Scriptures don't say what kind of a tree it was, but I believe it was a supernatural tree placed there by God Himself. It probably wasn't an entire tree, but maybe just a branch, as the NLT describes it. Whatever it was, Moses took it and threw it into the water. Maybe that old branch just stuck there in the ground of the riverbed, not looking like much. Then all of a sudden, perhaps, the waters around it started turning clear, and after a few minutes, the dirty, polluted, bitter waters had become sweet and clean.

Are you getting the message? Whatever relationship problem you're having can be made sweet if you will take the cross and plant it right in the middle of the problem. What was bitter can become the sweetest thing in your life, and what was muddied can become so clear that your life becomes a witness to others.

Interestingly, God revealed Himself as Jehovah-Rapha, the Lord our Healer, at the waters of Marah. Look at verse

26: "If you diligently heed the voice of the Lord your God and do what is right in His sight, give ear to His commandments and keep all His statutes, I will put none of the diseases on you which I have brought on the Egyptians. For I am the Lord who heals you."

I don't think it's an accident that this verse follows the account of the bitter waters of Marah. There is a definite relationship between bitterness and physical health. Doctors will tell you that if you allow bitterness to take root in your life, it will affect your physiology. It disrupts your body chemistry and causes you to be more susceptible to disease. Bitterness harbored in your spirit has a definite effect on your body, but when you allow the cross to heal the bitterness and restore relationships, then God can move on your behalf as your healer.

Healing Relationships Through the Power of the Cross

In Galatians, Ephesians, Philippians, and Colossians, Paul presents four various shades of understanding about the cross and how it heals relationships. Each epistle addresses a specific aspect of what the cross means and what the death of Jesus obtained in order that we could walk in peace and freedom in all our relationships.

Death to Self (Gal. 2:20)

At the beginning of Galatians 2, the Bible records a disagreement between Peter and Paul. We tend to think that everyone in the early church was totally saved and sanctified, never facing the trials that plague us. We think they must have been perfect, having lived and walked with Jesus in the flesh. However, the early church had problems, just like we do. It was composed of imperfect people who struggled with the same issues of the heart that you and I struggle with. That's one thing I appreciate about the Bible: it tells the "good, the bad, and the ugly," never sugarcoating the truth. In that way, we can relate to it easily.

The second chapter of Galatians reveals the tension that developed in Peter and Paul's relationship when Peter acted in a hypocritical manner. In Antioch, Peter was freely eating and fellowshipping with the uncircumcised Gentile Christians until some Jewish brothers from James arrived. Then he suddenly turned his back on the Gentile Christians, refusing to eat with them because he feared what the Jewish brothers might say. His action caused the other Jewish Christians present to follow his example, denying fellowship with the Gentile Christians.

Paul immediately recognized the hypocrisy taking place and boldly called Peter on the carpet for it. This is how he described the confrontation: "Now when Peter had come to Antioch, I withstood him to his face, because he was to be blamed" (Gal. 2:11). That's pretty straightforward, isn't it? Paul blamed Peter and confronted him about it. If Peter was like must of us (and I'm sure he was), he didn't take kindly to Paul's words. In essence, Paul was telling him, "You're being a hypocrite, man. You'd better get your act together!"

Even in the midst of such strong contention, I believe Paul was committed to keeping the relationship right and not letting the disagreement separate him from his brother in Christ. Look how he expresses it in verse 20: "I have been crucified with Christ; it is no longer I who live, but Christ lives in me; and the life which I now live in the flesh I live by faith in the Son of God, who loved me and gave Himself for me."

In this statement, Paul touches on the first critical aspect of bringing healing to any relationship: a willingness to die to self. Self and ego are at the root of all relational conflicts. Each of us has a natural instinct for self-preservation at the core of our being. We generally tolerate others, but only as long as they don't get in the way of what we want. You know how it is: You're moving in a certain direction at a certain speed, like a train on a track, when all of a sudden, along comes some old "cow" that decides to straddle the track. You get angry because now you're going to have to put the brakes on and stop your forward progress. Some of you don't let that cow slow you down one bit, though. You throw a little more wood on the fire and just knock the old cow out of the way!

That's the way so many of us do in our relationships. Some "cow" gets in our way, but we don't want to stop, so it's just full steam ahead—no matter who is in the way or who gets hurt in the process. It's an attitude of "It's my way or the highway." You might get your way with that kind of attitude, but you'll leave behind a string of broken, damaged relationships in the process.

If relationships in your life are going to work, you are going to have to die to self. Death to self means no longer having a personal agenda to promote. It means a willingness to look at things from someone else's perspective. It sounds so simple—and really it is—but it's something so few people actually do.

You might be thinking, "Not me, Pastor. I don't have a problem with self." Well, what about when you're sitting around with your family watching TV? What happens with the remote control? Do you get to decide what everyone else watches? That's why some of you have so many TVs in your house: because everyone wants his own remote so he can watch what he wants! We don't say, "What would you like to watch tonight?" Instead we say, "Give me that remote; I know what I want to watch!"

Galatians 5:24 continues the theme of dying to self: "And those who are Christ's have crucified the flesh with its passions and desires." Verse 14 of Chapter 6 KJV says, "But God forbid that I should glory, save in the cross of our Lord

Jesus Christ, by whom the world is crucified unto me, and I unto the world." In other words, these two verses taken together state a decision to die to the world's opinions, to personal agenda, and even to the world's applause. When that is your attitude, you can bear criticism, and the accolades of man mean very little to you. Whether someone gets upset with you or strokes your ego is irrelevant when you have died to self and glory only in the cross of Christ. *Nothing* affects, moves, disappoints, rattles, confuses, disrupts, hinders, or dismays when you are crucified with Christ. You are dead to all external influences because you are dead to self.

When you look at it that way, it's easy to see that when you're in conflict with someone, it's because there's some agenda you're pushing and promoting that the other person isn't cooperating with. This is the power struggle that occurs in so many families, churches, and nations, but every one of them could be immediately settled by the cross. The bitter hostility between people would turn sweet if both parties would allow the Holy Spirit to put self to death.

Forgiveness of the Past (Eph. 2:12–14)
The second way that the cross brings healing in relationships is by neutralizing bitter memories. Paul knew all about this, too. During his day, there were marked distinctions between Jews and Gentiles, and these distinctions were not automatically erased as Christianity unfolded. Jews and Gentiles had big-time racial differences and prejudices. Jews wouldn't even eat with Gentiles, for fear of being defiled.

Paul knew that the cross demolished all barriers that separated individuals and even groups of people. In verse 12 of Ephesians 2, he said, "At that time [in the past] you were without Christ, being aliens from the commonwealth of Israel and strangers from the covenants of promise, having no hope and without God in the world." Verses 13 and 14 continue: "But now in Christ Jesus you who once were far off have been brought near by the blood of Christ. For He Himself is our peace, who has made both one, and has broken down the middle wall of separation." Verse 16 wraps it up: "That He might reconcile them both to God in one body through the cross, thereby putting to death the enmity."

The cross has the power to bring two irreconcilable people together. I don't care how long the problem has been going on, how deep the hurt is, or how ingrained the deeds of the past are in your mind. When you embrace the power of the cross, that means you can let go of the past, with all it entails. It means you let sleeping dogs lie and don't keep waking them up. You'd never let your cat kill a rat and leave it on your laundry room floor, would you? No, you'd quickly sweep that mess out of there in a hurry before it smelled up your entire house. That's what you have to do with the hurts of the past: sweep them out the door before they cause everything in your life to stink!

Some of you haven't grasped that yet. You "forgive" someone who hurt you, and you do okay for a week or two. Then you disappear for a few minutes and come back with the same old junk dredged up. Some of you have been talking about the same old hurt for years now. It's time to let it go once and for all. You've got to forget the past by bringing it to the cross and letting the Lord bring reconciliation. If the waters in your life are bitter because of past failures and hurts, throw the cross right into the middle of it, and watch the Lord turn it sweet.

In our passage in Ephesians, Paul, talking about Jews and Gentiles, said that through Christ both groups had access to the Father through the Spirit (v. 18). The Spirit breaks through the wall of hostility that separates people. The problem is, so many of us don't want the wall removed; we're content to be like ice cubes in a tray. We stay in our separate compartments, aloof from and not touching anyone else. We become God's "frozen chosen," all because someone hurt us and we erected barriers to try to protect ourselves. We don't want to have anything to do with the one who offended us.

You know how it is; you might have done it yourself when someone hurt you. You give him the cold shoulder or decide to use the silent treatment on him. You think you'll make him suffer a while, but before you know it, the episode drags on and on. You're miserable, but you don't want to give in.

I remember Brother John Osteen talking about how his wife, Dodie, said something to him one time that offended him, so he decided to stop talking to her. It continued for two days, three days—she had really offended the "great one"! He woke up one morning and couldn't find his wife. He was concerned, because it's hard to give your wife the silent treatment if she's not around! He looked for her in the backyard, and he looked in the bathroom; he went all over the house searching for his wife. He couldn't find her. Then he started calling her name: "Dodie, Dodie!" Suddenly as he was walking down the hallway, Dodie came from behind and jumped on his back, put her arms around his neck, and said, "I'm not getting down until you talk to me!"

It's kind of hard to continue the silent treatment after that, but I learned something from Brother Osteen's transparency and willingness to share his imperfections. We've got to bring our issues to the cross and resolve them with whomever we are in conflict with before they cause us to freeze and harden our hearts toward the person. Problems not dealt with cause all kinds of grief and difficulty, but when you allow the power of the cross to touch you, you "melt together" with other people. No longer are you cold and hardhearted, apart from everyone else. You become willing and even desire to see your life melted and molded with others.

Desire to Serve (Phil. 2:1–11)

Philippians is the third epistle that provides a little more insight into the cross. It's sort of like turning a picture around to get a better or different view of it. First, we looked at Galatians and saw that the cross means dying to self. Then, we looked at the cross from the angle of Ephesians and saw that we have to let go of the past and let the cross heal it. Finally, when we look at the cross from the angle of Philippians, we find that the cross means a desire to serve. This is how Paul said it in Philippians 2:1–4:

> Therefore if there is any consolation in Christ, if any comfort of love, if any fellowship of the Spirit, if any affection and mercy, fulfill my joy by being like-minded, having the same love, being of one accord, of one mind. Let nothing be done through selfish ambition or conceit, but in lowliness of mind let each esteem others better than himself. Let each of you look out not only for his own interests, but also for the interests of others.

The power of the cross in relationships is never more evident than when we begin serving our enemies. That is a true miracle and shows a heart healed and free of the past. I realize that's not the way the world thinks. The world says, "That person hurt me. I'm not about to serve him. He should be serving me—he's caused me so much heartache, pain, and frustration. I'm not about to do anything for him!" You can keep that kind of attitude if you want, but that's why the water of your life is so bitter. You'll never be free until you allow the cross to totally change you from the inside out, helping you to think of others and their needs over your own.

If anyone ever had the right to think of Himself and His position, it was Jesus. The Son of God possessed all the treasures of heaven, yet willingly surrendered everything He had for our sakes. Jesus, "being in the form of God, did not consider it robbery to be equal with God, but made Himself of no reputation, taking the form of a bondservant, and coming in the likeness of men. And being found in appearance as a man, He humbled Himself and became obedient to the point of death, even the death of the cross" (Phil. 2:6–8).

Think about it! The Lord of the universe was willing to humble Himself to come to this depraved earth of ours and die naked before the world. The Lord and Creator of us all, the One who made the very tree that He hung upon, was willing to forgo all the glory of heaven to die an ignominious death on a cursed tree of shame and degradation.

Doesn't that help keep your problems in perspective? If Jesus could forgive those who betrayed and killed Him, can't you forgive your husband for not being the perfect mate? Can't you forgive that wayward child who doesn't appreciate all you've done for him? And what about the "Judas" in your life? Jesus forgave His Judas. On the night of the Last Supper, He washed all His disciples' feet, including the feet of the one who would betray Him. How do you think He felt, washing the feet of Peter, James, John, and the others and then coming to Judas? Regardless of personal feelings, He washed the feet of the traitor. That is the ultimate power of the cross.

Romans 12:20 says to give your enemy drink if he is thirsty, to feed him if he is hungry. Never are you allowed to get back at those who have hurt you. If anyone needs to be punished or vengeance exacted, God will do it in His way and time. That's not for you to know or even be concerned about. Your only role is to die to self, forgive, and then serve. You cannot let yourself be overcome by evil, but instead you must overcome evil with good.

What would it be like if you started serving others instead of worrying about what others were or were not doing for you? That's something my wife and I love to do. We are in a perpetual contest to see which one can serve the other the most. Now, I mess up every now and then and let her serve me more, but really, we look for ways to bless the other. That's the essence of love, and that's what Jesus demonstrated by His life and death.

Any relationship will improve when you decide to take the role of a servant. Are you mad about your neighbor's leaves blowing all over your yard? Go rake them up for him and set them by the side of the road. Does your coworker irritate you to no end? Make a conscious effort to find the good in her and concentrate on that. Does your mother keep treating you like a child? Honor and respect her, and be glad she cares enough to still want to be involved in your life. It doesn't matter which relationship it is; you can take the ultimate act of service—Jesus' death on the cross—and put it smack-dab in the middle of your relationship and watch the bitter waters turn sweet.

Victory over "Arguments" (Col. 2:14)

Satan is the accuser of the brethren. He sows discord, accusing others' motives, actions, and thoughts. All his work is based upon legal accusations resulting from our personal failures. But notice Colossians 2:13–14 NLT: "You were dead because of your sins and because your sinful nature was not yet cut away. Then God made you alive with Christ. He forgave all our sins. He canceled the record that contained the charges against us. He took it and destroyed it by nailing it to Christ's cross."

I like that word *cancel* in verse 14. Jesus canceled all the legitimate charges of sin against us so Satan would have no grounds to accuse us. If you don't know that, however, it's like credit card charges that come rolling around at the end of the month. You went out during the month and bought all kinds of things. You might have had lots of fun using the card, eating out and buying all kinds of clothes. Then the end of the month comes, and it's time to pay for what you did. You look at the statement and can't believe all the charges, but you made every one of them.

Satan keeps a running total of your sins, and he wants to whip them out and shove them under your nose every chance he gets. He'll try to whisper in your ear, "Remember that time you lied to get out of trouble?" Or, "I know what you looked at on the computer last week!" He'll try to dig up anything you ever did or thought about doing and use it against you. But when you understand that the cross has canceled all those accusations against you, you realize that Satan no longer has room to maneuver and bring you into conflict. The "fire is out" and the "wood is wet"!

When a debt had been canceled in Jesus' day, the proclamation of its payment was physically nailed upon the property. Then it was known that the property was free and clear, paid in full. When Jesus died on the cross, He once and for all canceled the certificate that contained the list of your sins. Even though you were guilty of them, He took that list and nailed it to the cross, right between his hands and the nails.

The devil is holding a "mortgage" against you, and he wants you to pay the debt for every sin you ever committed. He will stop at nothing to drag you to an eternity in hell with him and all his demons. If you listen to him every time he brings up something you've done or something someone has done to you, you'll allow him to erect arguments in your mind. Some children entertain thoughts about how mean and unreasonable their parents are, and before you know it, they've embraced an argument against them. A wife may start dwelling on some shortcoming of her husband, and soon she sees nothing good in him—only the bad. When you have thoughts like that, realize what the devil is doing and immediately bring those unruly thoughts to the cross so that you can have victory.

I heard a story one time about a man who lived on the prairie in Kansas. One day there was a huge fire, and everyone was evacuating. This man was reluctant to leave because he owned quite a bit of land, so he decided to stay. Before the fire reached his land, he went out and burned an area around his holdings. He set it on fire but controlled the burn. When that ferocious fire came roaring across the plain, it went racing right up to the edge of his property and stopped. There was no fuel left for the fire to consume, and it had nowhere to go. That vicious prairie fire never touched the man's house.

In Christ, your sin, iniquity, and failures have already been "burned over." The devil no longer has any fuel he can use against you. That long list of failures he wants to wave at you has already been taken by Jesus and irrevocably nailed to the cross, right between His hands and the wood. When the devil pops up his head and tries to wreak havoc in your relationships, he's got nothing he can put his hands on. It's already been nailed to the cross and marked "paid in full"!

Through the canceling of the charges against you, "God disarmed the evil rulers and authorities. He shamed them publicly by his victory over them on the cross of Christ" (v. 15 NLT). All relational hindrances and arguments have already been placed under your feet, and Satan has no authority to destroy the relationships in your life.

The power of the cross to heal relationships is available to anyone who will take advantage of it. First, decide to die to yourself and your carnal desires. Second, ask the Lord to help you to forgive and forget all the hurts of the past. Third, acknowledge that real power and change will come into your relationships only when you allow the Lord to give you the desire to serve others, even your enemies. And fourth, believe and act upon the truth that Christ has nailed to the cross every relational problem and obstacle so that you can have victory in Him.

That's how you turn the bitter waters sweet. That's how you restore every damaged relationship. That's how you learn to trust again after you've been let down year after year. The power in the cross is real. It's not some fairy tale told to make you feel good. It is more real than any battle you're facing or any long-standing problem you're enduring. Your part is simply to receive it in your heart and begin living it in your life. And when you do, the power in the cross will truly make all things new!

Chapter 3
Power over Discouragement

In addition to the power of the cross to set you free from bondage and to heal your relationships, the cross can give you victory over discouragement. From the beginning of time, man has struggled with a less than perfect life, and that will forever be the case as long as the earth continues. Even though we may be Christians and love the Lord with all our hearts, we're still going to experience trials and tribulations in this life on earth. That's just the way it is, and denying that truth doesn't make it any less so. The question isn't, *Am I going to have trials?* but rather the question is, *How am I going to handle them?*

When you are faced with a trial, you are faced with a choice. You can grow discouraged and throw in the towel, or you can call upon the power of the cross to help you overcome. Only a heavenly perspective will permit you to look beyond the present circumstances to the victory that is possible through Christ.

Look and Live! (Num. 21:4–9)

In Numbers 20–21, we see a story about the people of Israel and how they handled discouragement. As Israel neared the Promised Land and the end of their long journey, the land of Edom stood before them. The Edomites were their relatives descended through Esau, so when the Israelites came to the Edomites' land, they petitioned for permission to pass peacefully through (Num. 20:14-17). To Israel's surprise and dismay, Edom refused to grant permission. Right when they were on the verge of entering the Promised Land, their own relatives suddenly impeded their progress.

They couldn't fight their kin, so they had no choice but to take a detour around Edom to get to the Promised Land. All they would have needed was for Edom to grant permission, and then they could have made a beeline right into their land; but Edom would not cooperate. So a detour was inevitable.

Nobody likes a detour. We all want to go where we want in as little time as possible. Have you ever been driving toward a destination only to find the usual route closed and a detour in place? If you're like me, you didn't like it, and you probably grumbled a bit about it. Your plan was disturbed and you had to make an adjustment, even though you didn't want to. You were forced to detour.

"The people became very discouraged" (v. 4).

That's what faced Moses. He had to tell everybody that they were going to take a detour east to go into the Promised Land that was directly north of them. At this point, Israel had already been walking in the wilderness for thirty years, and they were physically and emotionally ready to move into the Promised Land. Suddenly this unforeseen detour came up, and their response, though understandable, was not the best one: "Then they journeyed from Mount Hor by the Way of the Red Sea, to go around the land of Edom; and the soul of the people became very discouraged on the way. And the people spoke against God and against Moses" (Num. 21:4-5a).

The literal translation of the Hebrew word for *discouraged* means to "cut off." In other words, we could say the people of Israel got hacked off! They were hot and angry and discouraged with the whole sorry mess. There they were, all set to go forward, and then they were told they were going to have to take a detour. As a result, many of them grew impatient and discouraged.

Detours are unavoidable. From time to time, you're going to encounter things that are going to force you to come to a full stop in your tracks and take what appears to be an unnecessary detour. Maybe you've been struggling to get out of debt, and about the time it seems like you're making a little bit of progress . . . wham! You're hit from behind with a huge, expected expense. Or, maybe it seems like your spouse is finally getting right with God, but then it doesn't last more than a week or two. The list is endless as to the things that can disappoint you in life.

You can try rebuking that thing in Jesus' name until you're blue in the face, but it's not the devil interfering with your life, but God allowing you to face the trial so He can build endurance in you. If you don't see it, though, you become discouraged and hacked off with whomever you perceive as the cause of your detour.

"And the people spoke against God and Moses" (v. 5).

That's exactly what Israel did. Moses was trying his best to lead those rebellious people despite the unexpected turn of events, but they not only refused to cooperate, but they also decided that God and Moses were to blame for their problem! "And the people spoke against God and against Moses: 'Why have you brought us up out of Egypt to die in the wilderness? For there is no food and no water, and our soul loathes this worthless bread' " (Num. 21:5). Suddenly they forgot every miracle God had done for them and every time Moses had demonstrated God's power on their behalf. They wanted someone to blame, and Moses was the scapegoat.

First, they told Moses, "We're tired of you and your leadership. You've brought us nothing but trouble from the day we followed you out of Egypt. We are not the least bit happy with the way things have turned out, and it's all your fault." They were ruled by their emotions and riding that emotional roller coaster that had them dancing on the shores of the Red Sea after their mighty deliverance from Pharaoh followed by grumbling and complaining when they didn't have water a few days later (Ex. 15:20, 24). That was their pattern, and unfortunately, that's the pattern for many of us, too. We shout and jump when God does what we want, but we doubt and complain the minute things don't go our way.

Israel's complaint didn't stop with criticizing Moses. After attacking him, they then had the audacity to blame God for their situation. It was like they were saying, "Lord, we're tired of You and Your leadership. We don't like the way You're doing things. You're not doing a very good job, so we need to take matters into our own hands."

That is quite a dangerous position to take: blaming God and grumbling against Him and His leaders. But that's exactly what Israel did. They didn't hesitate to tell God how much they loathed His provision for them. They said, "We're sick of this manna. We've been eating manna burgers, "mannacotti," and every manna dish you can imagine. We've done everything we can do with this manna, and we're sick of it." What nerve! Now maybe they did get tired of the manna, but can you imagine their complaining to God about the very thing He had miraculously provided to sustain them?

Some of us are just like that. We're not content with the way God has provided for us. In our minds, He should be doing more. We don't have everything we want right when we want it, so we think God is to blame. Some of us don't hesitate to just go ahead and blurt out every evil thought that comes into our minds.

Murmuring and speaking against God is a very dangerous thing. God often allows us to go through circumstances that He knows are for our own good; however, we tend to react to those circumstances with a bad case of "garbage mouth." When we gripe and complain, however, we are destroying ourselves, just like Israel did. Little did they know that as they carried on with their murmuring, God was listening and taking account of everything that was coming out of their mouths. They didn't know that their tongues were destroying them and opening the floodgates of evil in their lives.

James 3:6 tells us that "the tongue is a fire, a world of iniquity. The tongue is so set among our members that it defiles the whole body, and sets on fire the course of nature; and it is set on fire by hell." Although it is quite small, it can do great damage. It can defile your entire body and is itself set on fire from hell.

The devil is the one who works with your mind when you're faced with a trying situation. He's constantly prodding you to speak against people, yourself, or God. He tells you it's your "right" to do so, but if you listen to Him, you're going to light a fire that you can't outrun. That's how dangerous an unbridled tongue is.

You might think, "Oh, a few words won't hurt anything, and I'll feel better after I get things off my chest." So you throw a spark here and a spark there. But the fire caused by your words catches on so quickly and moves so fast, it's almost explosive. Before you know what's happened, the fire has engulfed you, and you're trapped in it. By your spoken words, you've destroyed God's hedge of protection around you and made yourself vulnerable to the enemy.

"So the Lord sent fiery serpents among the people" (v. 6).

Look what happened to Israel: "So the Lord sent fiery serpents among the people, and they bit the people; and many of the people of Israel died" (Num. 21:6). Snakes started showing up in the camp of Israel after their bitter complaining against God. I believe the snakes had been present in the land all the time, but their activity against the people had been restrained until Israel gave vent to their complaining. At that point, God lifted the hedge of protection and the snakes began slithering into the camp.

Maybe it was at night when no one was aware of what was going on, or maybe it was in broad daylight; the Bible doesn't tell us exactly when the snakes appeared. But appear they did, and with a vengeance they began biting the people. It must have been an awful scene: people screaming and trying to get away from the snakes, but unable to escape them. There were snakes in the tents and snakes in the open. Everywhere the people turned, there were snakes. People began to scream, not only as they were bitten but also as the fear of being bitten gripped them. These were poisonous snakes, so now people began dying. Oh, the wailing and weeping that must have taken place! But it was too late. Their sin of complaining and murmuring against God was reaping a bitter harvest of death.

That's the way the devil always operates. Once you give in to discouragement and let your tongue loose, saying anything you please, you're giving an open invitation to the devil to enter your life and wreak havoc. You might open the door just a crack, but he'll not stop until he has forced the door all the way open and has total access to your life.

The people of Israel were in trouble and knew it. Immediately they turned to Moses for help, the same man they had just gotten through blasting. They said, "We have sinned, for we have spoken against the Lord and against you; pray to the Lord that He take away the serpents from us" (Num. 21:7). Moses' response is recorded in the last part of the verse: "So Moses prayed for the people." The long-suffering leader who had been reviled and slandered now prayed for the ungrateful Israelites, and God told him what to do: "Then the Lord said to Moses, 'Make a fiery serpent, and set it on a pole; and it shall be that everyone who is bitten, when he looks at it, shall live' " (Num. 21:8).

"Make a fiery serpent, and set it on a pole" (v. 8).
Isn't it interesting that the exact thing that was causing the suffering—the fiery serpent—was the thing that God instructed Moses to make a model of? The fiery serpents were the problem, and now the form of a serpent was the answer. This is the first and best picture of the cross in the Old Testament. Like the serpent on the pole, the cross and the death that it represents is yet the instrument of eternal life.

Moses obeyed God and constructed the brass serpent. The brass serpent was then lifted high on a pole in the camp for every victim of snakebite to see. It would have taken a while to fashion, so in the meantime, people were continuing to die. When the brass serpent was finally ready, Moses probably sent word through the camp, telling the people, "I know it sounds crazy, but just do what I say and you'll be okay. If a snake bites you, quit looking at yourself and rubbing the injury and feeling sorry for yourself. Stop bawling and squalling, and just look at the brass serpent on the pole."

Just look at it! That's what they had to do. They had to fix their eyes on the symbol of their sin in order for the power of God to flow through their bodies and reverse the curse. In the same way, when you fix your eyes upon Jesus' death on the cross, you find the cure for every bad attitude that you have. If you take your eyes off the cross, however, the flow of power stops, and you lapse back into your old ways of doing things.

The serpent that Moses made represented Jesus. It's hard to imagine a serpent as representative of Jesus, but when He hung on the cross, He *was* sin, spiritually speaking. We see a man hanging on the cross, but God saw sin hanging there in all its ugliness. All the junk and wickedness of the world was piled upon Jesus on the cross, and spiritually, He looked the part.

If one of the Israelites got bitten by a snake, he had to fix his gaze upon the brass serpent if he wanted to live. Even if he was short of breath, his heart pounding, and a fever raging through his body from the effect of the snakebite, he still had to concentrate on the serpent. He couldn't just glance at it every now and then; he had to stare at it with all his might, locking his gaze upon it and refusing to look to the left or to the right. Only then would he be healed.

As he concentrated upon the symbol of his sin, life began to flow back into his body. He probably began to breathe a little easier. Then he may have felt the pain leaving his joints. The fever subsided, and he began to feel like he might make it. As he kept his focus on the serpent, all the poison and death in his body suddenly began to reverse.

What a beautiful picture of how to overcome discouragement! I don't know where you are today—what's distracted or discouraged you. Maybe you have problems in your family or on your job. You might have a bad case of the "mulley-grubs" and the "can't help its," but if you're not keeping your eyes on Jesus and the mighty delivering power of the cross, you're looking at the wrong thing. If you'll keep your focus on Him, little by little you'll get better, just like the Israelites did. The pain and discouragement will start to ease, and life will flow back into your heart and spirit.

The Power of Looking at Jesus

Deliverance from Self-Pity (Heb. 12:1–2)

Like the Old Testament, the New Testament talks about keeping our eyes on Jesus. Hebrews 11:32–40 is a roll call of those who endured by faith. They went through awful trials, tribulations, and afflictions, but they endured by faith. Who could fail to be moved by the eloquent words of Scripture (Heb. 11:35–38) in describing these stalwart men and women of God?

> Others were tortured, not accepting deliverance, that they might obtain a better resurrection. Still others had trial of mockings and scourgings, yes, and of chains and imprisonment. They were stoned, they were sawn in two, were tempted, were slain with the sword. They wandered about in sheepskins and goatskins, being destitute, afflicted, tormented—of whom the world was not worthy. They wandered in deserts and mountains, in dens and caves of the earth.

Hebrews 12:1 reminds us of these faithful witnesses and encourages us to draw strength from their example. They endured the most dreadful things imaginable, but they never lost their faith. Imprisoned, stoned, sawn in two, killed by the sword—the treatment was irrelevant to these heroes of the faith who stood firm regardless of what happened to them. These were men and women willing to sacrifice everything—including their lives—for Christ's sake, and some of us have the nerve to complain that our house is too small or our car is the wrong color!

Somewhere along the line our perspective has gotten skewed. We think if everything doesn't go perfectly, just the way we planned, then something must be wrong. We get discouraged over the smallest things and are ready to backslide when someone doesn't speak to us at church. If, however, we look at the examples from Scripture and even examples from people living in our day, we'll see how true faith and knowledge of Christ's power can sustain us through anything.

The Power of the Cross

You may remember the story of Martin and Gracia Burnham, missionaries to the Philippines. In May of 2001, they, along with several other people, were kidnapped from a resort in the Philippines where they had gone for an anniversary celebration. Their Muslim captors kept them for a year, until June 7, 2002, when a rescue effort was attempted. During the ensuing gunfight, Gracia suffered a shot to the leg, and Martin was killed.

If anyone had a right to be discouraged and feel sorry for herself, it would be this brave woman. She had gone to the Philippines as a missionary with her husband, had served God faithfully in that capacity for fifteen years, had lived in captivity as a prisoner for a year, only to have the whole thing end with her husband being killed. She could have become bitter, angry with God and determined to never serve Him again. By all outward circumstances, it certainly looked like God had let her down. But that is not what she did. She continued serving God and travels around today declaring the goodness of the Lord. She has written a book, *In the Presence of My Enemies,* chronicling her captivity and sharing what she learned. She has become stronger as a result of her trial, even though she suffered great loss. She is an example of a person with a living faith that has carried her through one of the greatest trials imaginable.

Paul says in Hebrews 12:1–2 that since we have this great cloud of witnesses to encourage us, we can now "lay aside every weight, and the sin which so easily ensnares us, and... run with endurance the race that is set before us, looking unto Jesus, the author and finisher of our faith, who for the joy that was set before Him endured the cross, despising the shame, and has sat down at the right hand of the throne of God." Whom are we supposed to be looking at? Jesus! Not the bank, our employer, the stock market, or any of the other innumerable things clamoring for our attention—but solely Jesus! When we look at Him crucified upon the cross, it reminds us that we really haven't gone through anything. If He was willing to endure that terrible death, then surely we can put up with the things that we're going through.

Paul reminds us that Christ is our example in endurance. The cross, as awful as it was, was only a door to the resurrection. I know you're going through problems, difficulties, and circumstances. I know it's tempting to feel sorry for yourself and find someone to blame for your situation. When you do that, however, you've gotten your eyes on the wrong thing. You're looking at another person or the impossibility of the circumstance instead of the power of the cross to help you endure.

Turn your vision to the cross and join your voice with hymn-writer Isaac Watts in proclaiming:

> When I survey the wondrous cross
> On which the Prince of Glory died,
> My richest gain I count but loss,
> And pour contempt on all my pride.

Look at the cross and see what the Savior endured for you. Gaze upon those nail-pierced hands and wounded side. Look at the crown of thorns thrust viciously into His lovely head. Look at the cross, and your own sufferings will pale in comparison.

Hebrews 12:3 KJV begins with two startling words: "Consider Him." That's the problem: You're considering everybody else but Him. "Consider him that endured such contradiction of sinners against himself, lest ye be wearied and faint in your minds." Where do you experience the feeling of discouragement? In your mind! The devil attacks your mind when you're going through trials and tries to get you to look at the problem at hand, but the Lord says, "Look and live!" The remedy for all of it is to turn your attention back to the price Jesus paid on the cross of suffering.

When you get your eyes back on the cross, you say, "Hey, this stuff that I'm facing is nothing! So what that I've got a car with cloth seats instead of leather? You know what? It really isn't such a big deal!" As you start realizing the smallness of your problem, supernatural endurance comes upon you. Self-pity is driven out, and faith and right thinking come in.

Self-pity is a dangerous attitude because it keeps you looking at yourself. It's an attitude of "Poor me. Nobody's seen the trouble I've seen. Nobody cares. Nobody ever thinks about me. Nobody ever calls me. I might as well give up." Thinking like that keeps your focus on yourself and your problems, but the One who died on the cross would say to you today: "Don't you dare give up! After what I've been through for you? Don't you dare give up! Look to Me and take the power I offer you to overcome. Look to Me and live!"

Deliverance from Self-Defensiveness (1 Pet. 2:21)

When we keep our eyes on the cross, not only can we be set free from self-pity, but we also can get free from self-defensiveness. Let's look at how this is accomplished. The Bible says in 1 Peter 2:21 KJV, "For even hereunto were ye called: because Christ also suffered for us, leaving us an example, that ye should follow his steps." Peter reminds us to follow in the steps of Christ, and we know right where Christ's steps led Him: to the cross! That tells me that if I follow Christ, my steps are also going to lead me to the cross. Peter continues in the next two verses: "Who did no sin, neither was guile found in his mouth: Who, when he was reviled, reviled not again; when he suffered, he threatened not; but committed himself to him that judgeth righteously." That's our example.

If we were honest, most of us would have to admit that we don't want to follow Jesus to the cross, especially when someone has spoken badly about us or caused us suffering. We don't want to commit ourselves to the One who judges righteously; we want to take matters into our own hands. We're determined to protect ourselves from what we view as the attacks of others. That is our natural human tendency: to lash out and attack those who attack us.

When a person is defensive, he is always on guard, just waiting for somebody to try something. He's so used to being hurt that he jumps down the throat of anybody who even looks like he's going to attack him. It reminds me of those old Western movies with the sharpshooters whose hands are always hovering just above their guns. They're always walking around looking suspiciously at everyone, just waiting for someone to dare to draw against them. If anybody's hand goes down below his belt for any reason, that sharpshooter is ready. Quick as a flash, he drops his hand, whips out his weapon, and blasts the other person before he even knows what hit him.

That's how some of you are. You're wary of everyone and constantly monitoring everyone's movements, looks, and words. If you see someone across the room talking, you're convinced he's talking about you. If people don't smile and tell you good morning, you just know they're mad at you. You imagine all kinds of things because you've become so self-defensive. You're always looking over your shoulder for someone trying to take advantage of you. You've grown suspicious of everything, and you trust no one.

Self-defensiveness always causes problems in interpersonal relationships, but especially in a marriage. After speaking about how Christ was totally defenseless against those who persecuted Him, Peter, in 1 Peter 3, immediately begins talking about husbands and wives. I think it is so interesting that Peter moves into this discussion about marriage at this point. He begins the chapter with "Wives, likewise, be submissive to your own husbands, that even if some do not obey the word, they, without a word, may be won by the conduct of their wives." In verse 7 he addresses husbands: "Husbands, likewise, dwell with them with understanding, giving honor to the wife." Peter, in effect, is telling both husband and wife that they can't be touchy and defensive in their marriage. If the husband is not very considerate, the wife does not have the freedom to rant and rail at him, even though what he is doing may be very wrong. If she opts to get defensive about all the ways he is failing her, she might win the immediate battle, but eventually she'll lose the war. Similarly, husbands are to treat their wives with understanding, again forgoing the desire to get defensive when their wives say or do hurtful things.

It works both ways in a marriage. Husbands and wives have to learn to stay focused on the cross when they are suffering injustice in the marriage relationship. Peter shows us the solution in verses 8–9: "Finally, all of you be of one mind, having compassion for one another; love as brothers, be tenderhearted, be courteous; not returning evil for evil or reviling for reviling, but on the contrary blessing, knowing that you were called to this, that you may inherit a blessing."

This, of course, applies to any relationship, whether with children, employers, neighbors, relatives, or friends. The devil will do his utmost to stir up strife in your relationships. Sometimes people attack you for no apparent reason. You didn't do anything wrong that you know of, but yet they come after you with all claws out. Now the question you face is whether you are going to pull out the "gun" and start blasting away at anyone who crosses you or whether you are going to follow in the steps of Christ and go to the cross with the offense. When you take your eyes off the person and instead look to the cross, you take the focus off yourself and put it on Christ. Like the Israelites in the wilderness, you look and live. But the choice is yours.

Deliverance from Self-Focus (2 Cor. 5:14)

Self-focus is the third snake that tries to crawl into the camp to destroy us. We all tend to get so wrapped up in ourselves. Day and night, we focus on worldly pursuits. The more we possess, however, the more miserable we become. That's because getting entangled with the cares of this world eventually chokes out all sense of meaning and purpose. We get so caught up in the pursuit of earthly wealth and pleasures that pretty soon we stop ministering to people. We cease witnessing, like we did at first. Before you know it, we don't even think about sharing the Gospel with our next-door neighbor, much less with the billions abroad who do not know the Savior. We're so busy thinking about "me" and "mine" that we miss the entire purpose of why we are here to begin with.

When you begin thinking that your life isn't going exactly the way you want it, when things aren't turning out the way you had planned, when nothing seems right and everything seems wrong, that's the time to look at the cross. You may have problems, but not as many as Jesus faced. Yes, you may have enemies, but not like He did. You've got to take the focus off yourself and reorient yourself to what is truly important.

Paul spells it out for us in 2 Corinthians 5:14–15: "For the love of Christ compels us, because we judge thus: that if One died for all, then all died; and He died for all, that those who live should live no longer for themselves, but for Him who died for them and rose again." *Compel*—that's a strong word Paul uses. It means we have no choice. We *must* be focused on His love and death and what it means to our lives. It means that we no longer have the right to live for ourselves, because our lives belong to Christ, the Savior who died for us.

Paul had it right. He went through all kinds of problems in his life, but he said, "You know what? I never lose my focus on sharing the Gospel because every day I remember the cross. Although the Lord is not there anymore, I remember the terrible price He paid."

When I walk through a military cemetery and see the white crosses of the men and women who have died for our nation, I never fail to be moved and to realize afresh their total sacrifice. These were people cut down in the prime of life. They gave their lives for my sake and the sake of all the country. When I count the cost, I am overwhelmed with gratitude and with the determination that those brave men and women will not have died in vain. So I vote in every election that comes up. I inform myself of current events and do my best to be an exemplary citizen of my city, state, and nation. I pray for the country and its leaders. It's the least I can do when others have sacrificed such a high cost for my freedom.

The same holds true for the Gospel. When I come to the cross and realize the extent of the price that Jesus paid—the suffering of the stripes on His back, the piercing agony of the crown of thorns, the horrendous pain of the nails and spear—when I look at the price He paid to redeem the world, the very least I can do is to accept the ministry of reconciliation He has given me (2 Cor. 5:18). In other words, I've got to tell others that Jesus died for them. He poured out His last drop of blood as their Redeemer and mine. We could not pay that price, and He will not make it His business to tell others about it. He is the Redeemer, and we are the ambassadors.

People are a lot hungrier and more receptive to the Gospel than you might think. I remember more than twenty-five years ago when I was a missionary in Africa. I was with a brother named Rick Zachary, and a messenger came from a certain region in Nigeria to tell us that there were some villages that had not yet heard the Gospel and wanted someone to come share with them. This man offered to take us down the river that led to those villages.

The Power of the Cross

In my mind, I was thinking that we would be gone an hour or two, so Rick and I readily agreed to go. We climbed into the "boat," which was really nothing more than a canoe with a little trolling motor. Then I looked to sit down, and there was my seat: a small, narrow board that was really nothing more than a slat! It felt like I was sitting on a broom handle. I thought I could bear it for a little while, but then I made the mistake of asking, "How far is it to the villages?"

"Oh, it's far," the messenger answered, and he wasn't kidding. We passed the time by fighting off tsetse flies—you know, those flies that give you sleeping sickness! So there I was, the big man of God with my college degree, sitting on a broom handle and fighting for my life! I have to admit, I did not keep the best attitude. I was irritated and aggravated, and not a happy camper.

Nine hours later, we finally arrived at the village. I was tired and upset and had no idea what I would say. I certainly didn't feel like a very good missionary. As we pulled in to shore, however, I saw hundreds of people waiting on the riverbank. Our boat glided to the shore and stopped, and all these people let out a shout. I started feeling a little better.

Then they took our suitcases and grabbed us, literally pulling us along the main street. They were practically carrying us, so eager were they to hear what we had to say. They brought us up on a hill, probably about 10 feet high, and then demanded, "Preach the Gospel now!" I'll never forget the urgency in their voices as long as I live. "Preach the Gospel now!" They didn't want to wait until the next day. They had waited for our arrival all day, and now they would not be denied. So we preached to those desperate, hungry people who wanted to know the Savior, and when I gave the invitation, every hand in the village went up. Four hundred people gave their hearts to the Lord.

That's how it is in so many places around the world. People are just waiting for someone to come and give them the Gospel. I remember a story I heard one time about the late John Osteen. Brother Osteen was in Mexico, and some guy flagged down the car he was riding in. Brother Osteen lowered the window, and the man asked the interpreter in the car, "Does anybody in here know anything about the Gospel?"

Brother Osteen quickly answered, "I do; I'm a pastor."

The man replied, "Would you please come to our village? My people sent me to hear the Gospel and bring it back to them." The man had come two hours from the mountains to the main road, flagging down cars and trying to find someone who could tell him the Gospel.

They all traveled to the village, and when they arrived, the villagers rang a bell. All the farmers came running from their fields, and they sat on little benches, taking off their sombreros and wiping off the sweat. Brother Osteen told them the simple story of Jesus, and the whole village got saved.

Missionaries have always been moved by this sense of urgency to share the Gospel because they understand that they are ambassadors for Christ. In the nineteenth century, missionary Robert Moffat uttered his immortal words: "I have sometimes seen, in the morning sun, the smoke of a thousand villages, where no missionary has ever been." Inspired by Moffatt, David Livingstone, one of the most famous missionaries ever known, was compelled to take the Gospel to Africa, which was then a spiritually dark continent. He is but one of thousands of men and women throughout the ages who have accepted their responsibility to proclaim Christ.

Whether you realize it or not, you are indeed a missionary, just as surely as was David Livingstone, Richard Carey, Hudson Taylor, or any of the other greats in missionary history. Never take your eyes off the cross where Jesus died for all peoples and nations. When you keep your focus there, you'll feel that same compulsion to share Christ. You won't be afraid to talk about Jesus in the grocery store or at work. You'll run to tell your neighbors about Him, and you'll be looking for any and every opportunity to preach the Gospel.

When Christ spoke to Nicodemus about being born again, He focused on the cross as the secret: "And as Moses lifted up the serpent in the wilderness, even so must the Son of Man be lifted up, that whoever believes in Him should not perish but have eternal life" (John 3:14). Look and live, and let the cross set you free!

Chapter 4
Power over Temptation

In the first three chapters, we saw just how powerful the cross truly is, whether it's over bondage, relationships, or discouragement. Chapter 1 showed us that when we understand the power of the cross to set us free, we realize how truly invincible we are in Christ. The cross is our jubilee, the gateway from the wilderness of bondage into the paradise of freedom. No habit, addiction, infirmity, or weakness is too strong for the cross of Christ.

Chapter 2 showed us how the cross is like the tree Moses placed in the bitter waters of Marah to make them sweet. At the cross, we die to self, forget the past, learn to serve, and cancel Satan's arguments against us. The bitter circumstances and experiences of our lives become sweet when we bring them to the cross.

Chapter 3 unveiled the cross as the antidote to despair, discouragement, and defensiveness. When Israel murmured in the wilderness, they were bitten by snakes. Moses' brass serpent lifted high on a pole was a type of Christ, who heals us from self-pity and self-focus.

Finally, in this chapter we come to the power of the cross to overcome temptation. The cross represents separation from the world and gives us the strength and conviction to stand against everything that tries to entice us back into sin. It is a present help in times of trouble and difficulty. As wonderful as it is that Christ is able to forgive your past and free you from every bondage from the past, you've got to know that He is able and willing to help you *now!* Every day of your life, temptation will come—you can count on it—but when the power of the cross is operating in your life, you know that you can overcome it.

First Corinthians 10:13 says, "No temptation has overtaken you except such as is common to man; but God is faithful, who will not allow you to be tempted beyond what you are able, but with the temptation will also make the way of escape, that you may be able to bear it." Temptation *is* going to come; that's inevitable. However, if your vision of the cross is clear, you are going to find that the draw of sin grows weaker as the power of the cross grows stronger in your life.

Temptation in the Bible

If we look in the very beginning of the Bible, in the book of Genesis, we find the first account of temptation. It's a familiar story, of course, but it has much to teach us. The story of the fall of mankind centers around a tree, the Tree of the Knowledge of Good and Evil. Adam and Eve had been instructed that they must not eat of this tree (Gen. 2:16–17), and that was just fine with them—at first. Then one day the crafty serpent appeared, and the first temptation was dangled before them. You know the ending: Eve succumbed to the temptation and lured Adam into it. Immediately their eyes were opened and their innocence lost. The consequences of their action brought swift punishment from God, not only for them but also for all mankind.

Adam and Eve's sin began with something they viewed with their eyes. They saw the fruit, and it represented food, beautiful things, and power. In other words, it represented the world and all that it offers. Second John 2:16 says, "For all that is in the world—the lust of the flesh, the lust of the eyes, and the pride of life—is not of the Father but is of the world." That describes exactly what happened to Eve. She saw that the fruit was good for food (lust of the flesh); it was pleasant to the eyes (lust of the eyes); and she took it because she thought it would make her wise (pride of life). She yielded to the devil's temptation and reaped the awful consequences (Gen. 3:6–7).

The first man, Adam, was unable to resist temptation, and through him, sin entered the world. Jesus, who is called the second Adam, was everything that the first Adam was not. Matthew 4 records the epic struggle between good and evil when Satan went all out to tempt Jesus to sin in the wilderness. At the end of this encounter, Jesus, unlike the first Adam, emerged totally victorious.

The first thing the devil did was to attack Jesus' flesh. Jesus had been fasting for forty days, when suddenly the devil appeared and said, "See that stone? Turn it into bread and eat it. You're hungry, aren't you?" So the devil appealed to Christ's flesh, to his natural appetite for physical food (vv. 1–3).

Appetites are good, given to us by God. One of the signs of good health is a good appetite, and when you are sick, you generally lose your appetite. You also have natural desires for water and rest, and you even have a God-given sexual appetite. As created by God, all these things are good, but when an appetite becomes a driving force in your life, fueling your passions and becoming overly important, then in effect it becomes a god to you. Some people "worship" food. Others "worship" golf. Still others "worship" sleep. The list is limitless as to the things people give undue priority to in their lives. When something becomes a god to you, you're going to be constantly tempted in that area. Your flesh is going to crave it, and unless you know how to fight temptation, you're going to give in to it.

Jesus knew how to fight fleshly temptation, and He did this by countering the devil's words with God's words: "It is written: 'Man shall not live by bread alone, but by every word that proceeds from the mouth of God' " (Matt. 4:4). So Satan was stopped dead in his tracks.

Not to be deterred, however, the devil next tried to sway Jesus through the pride of life. When the devil brought Jesus to the pinnacle of the temple and told Him to throw Himself down, he was appealing to pride. He was saying in effect, "Come on, Jesus. You know who You really are. You can just throw Yourself down from here, snap Your fingers, and have the angels catch you." He even quoted Psalm 91 to Him, cloaking his evil temptation in Scripture. Jesus refused to take the bait, answering Satan with "It is written again, 'You shall not tempt the Lord your God' " (v. 6). He had no need to prove anything to anybody. He knew who He was and was secure in that.

On the devil's third attempt to get Jesus to sin, he showed Him all the kingdoms of the world and said, "All you've got to do is bow down and worship me and I'll give them to you." The glitz and glamour of the world was spread before Jesus' eyes, but He refused to give in to its allure (vv. 8–10). Once more He emerged victorious, declaring, "Away with you, Satan! For it is written, 'You shall worship the Lord your God, and Him only you shall serve.' " With that, the temptation was over and the devil departed (v. 11).

Jesus was tempted in the same three areas that Adam and Eve were tempted, and those are the same three areas where you will be tempted, too. The lust of the flesh, the lust of the eyes, and the pride of life—these are what constantly pull at you to yield to sin. The key to victory, as Jesus knew, is to refuse to eat of the fruit of the Tree of the Knowledge of Good and Evil and to turn to the knowledge of the cross, the Tree of Life.

From the time Christ was twelve years old, He knew He had a special call to fulfill. We don't know exactly when the full knowledge of His destiny was revealed to Him, but we do know that He embraced it fully. He knew before it ever happened that He would one day face the cross (Matt. 16:21). His disciples didn't understand it, and when He tried to speak of it, they didn't want to hear of such an awful thing. Peter vehemently opposed Jesus "and began to rebuke Him, saying, 'Far be it from You, Lord; this shall not happen to You!' " (v. 22). But Jesus knew His way was the way of the cross.

Some people say it was impossible for Christ to sin, that when the devil tempted Him in the wilderness, it was really no big deal. But that's not so. One of the most basic tenets of the Christian faith is that Jesus was fully God and fully man. As a man, He faced real temptations. He had to choose what He would do at those moments when Satan did everything in his power to make Him fall. If Satan could have caused Jesus to sin, he would have been victorious over Jesus and subsequently all who came after Him. Knowing this, Jesus faced the temptations squarely and was victorious over every single one. He was obedient to the Father in all things, even to the ultimate act of going to the cross. That view of the cross was the thing that kept Him from giving in to Satan's temptations. He knew His destiny, and He set His face like a flint to fulfill it.

Jesus, of course, is no longer on the cross. He laid down His life, rose from the dead, and is seated as victor in heaven. The victory won at the cross represents the way that you and I can be free from every temptation the devil throws at us. Let's look at this by starting with Philippians 3:17–19:

Brethren, join in following my example, and note those who so walk, as you have us for a pattern. For many walk, of whom I have told you often, and now tell you even weeping, that they are the enemies of the cross of Christ: whose end is destruction, whose god is their belly, and whose glory is in their shame—who set their mind on earthly things.

Paul warned the Philippian believers that some had compromised the cross and had begun to yield to the temptations of the flesh, making a god out of their appetites. They even gloried in their shame, because their minds had drifted from the cross and onto earthly things.

That's just the way many Christians are. They have drifted from the relationship found with God at the cross, and they've entertained the world and its false attraction. They've gotten involved in earthly things; that's all they think about. They don't even give a thought to the cross and what it means to their lives anymore; yet some of these same people wonder why they have such a difficult time resisting temptation.

Sin is too powerful for you to try to combat it with just your mind. Without a sustained focus on the cross and an awareness of your heavenly citizenship, you will continue to fall into patterns and habits of sin. As long as you keep your focus on earthly things, sin will continue to hold you in its grasp. When you turn to the cross and keep your focus there, however, sin cannot maintain its hold on you.

Conquering Temptation Through the Power of the Cross

Hebrews 6, 10, and 13 have three little phrases that can really help you overcome temptation. They are three simple phrases, but they contain a wealth of truth within them. The stage for these phrases is actually set in Hebrews 5:12: "For though by this time you ought to be teachers, you need someone to teach you again the first principles of the oracles of God; and you have come to need milk and not solid food."

Churches, unfortunately, are full of spiritual babies. These are Christians who have never gotten off the bottle, so to speak. They come to church each week and open their mouths for a little eyedropper bit of nourishment from the Word, but that's all they want. They get their little bit of nourishment and then live a compromised life all week. They never pick up the Bible and study it on their own; they're content to wait for Sunday to let the pastor feed them a little bit more milk.

Power over temptation begins with spiritual maturity. Paul knew that; that's why he was so concerned with spiritually weak believers. Christians who never progress from "milk" to "meat" never grow strong enough to resist temptation. They are stuck in spiritual infancy and are dependent on stronger Christians to help them along. They have failed to move on in the things of God.

Let us go on! (Heb. 6:1–6)

That's the first phrase that will really help you overcome temptation. At some point in your Christian life, you have to decide to go on in Christ. When I graduated from kindergarten, I didn't stop my education there. I didn't go to the second grade and say, "That's enough. I think I'll stop now." I went on through grade school and graduated from high school, and then my dad said, "You're going on!" So I went on to college and graduated from there, too.

You need to go on in your Christian faith. You can't just sit week after week in the pew, content with getting a little bit of spiritual milk. I heard someone say one time that a baby is cute sucking on a bottle, but when you have to part the whiskers to put the bottle in, it starts to get ugly! There's nothing attractive about a weak, milk-fed Christian who has never progressed past getting saved.

Hebrews 6:1–2 lists those doctrines that are foundational to the Christian life: "repentance from dead works and of faith toward God, of the doctrine of baptisms, of laying on of hands, of resurrection of the dead, and of eternal judgment." These six basic doctrines are something all believers should know, understand, and apply to their lives. Many churches have courses that teach basic doctrine and spiritual maturity to new Christians. These are designed to help people go on to maturity so that they can bear fruit for God and be strong enough to resist temptation.

That's exactly what we've done at Bethany. After a person comes to the Lord at our church, we immediately begin working with him to help him mature in Christ. First we enroll him in something we call the Journey. Here his understanding of salvation is solidified, he's water-baptized, and he's prepared for a weekend Encounter Retreat. On the Encounter Retreat, the new believer visits the cross, receiving forgiveness, cleansing, and freedom from every bondage of the past. It's a way for him to begin his Christian walk, fresh and clean.

After the Encounter Retreat, the person enrolls in follow-up classes. For seven weeks, he studies and learns more about how to live out his new commitment to Christ. Then he moves into three terms of the Discovery, where he can study doctrine and learn who he is in Christ. By this time, the expectation is that he will be a strong, stable Christian who is going on in the Lord.

We've learned that if a person will go on in his Christian walk and not stop in "first grade," he'll be strong and know how to resist when the devil comes along with his bag of temptation. He'll have the Word of God as his sword and be quite capable of defeating the enemy. If he fails to go on and is content just to be saved, he is going to find himself quite defenseless against the devil. He has no sword—only a Q-tip—to fight with! That's how weak and impotent he is.

The choice to go on or not go on is yours. If you choose to stop progressing in your Christian walk, however, it's only a matter of time before you'll start backsliding. Once you start backsliding, you're in great danger. Verses 4–6 of Hebrews 6 says, "For it is impossible for those who were once enlightened, and have tasted the heavenly gift, and have become partakers of the Holy Spirit, and have tasted the good word of God and the powers of the age to come, if they fall away, to renew them again to repentance, since they crucify again for themselves the Son of God, and put Him to an open shame."

This verse is talking about willful, gross sin that involves turning your back on Jesus after knowing the truth. It's not talking about losing your temper and blowing your horn at somebody at the red light. The intentional rejection of Jesus and all that He stands for is so grievous that it's just like you are nailing Jesus to the cross all over again. You are bringing shame to Him because you once proudly bore His name.

Nothing could be more horrible than that. It was bad enough that Christ endured the agony of the cross for those six hours on that Friday afternoon so long ago. To think that by your own spiritual immaturity or lack of self-control, you could in effect recrucify the Savior is absolutely appalling.

I realize, of course, that Paul is talking about a spiritual action. Jesus physically died on the cross once and once only. Calvary is a finished work. Paul is emphasizing that when you leave the doctrine of Christ and go off into all kinds of ungodliness, you are holding Christ up again to open shame.

Think about your children. If they do something wrong in the public eye, it brings shame and embarrassment to you, because they bear your name. You still love them and you're pained that they have to go through the thing, but you are also deeply hurt and embarrassed by it. Your child's name in the paper for drunk driving, your daughter having a baby out of wedlock, a child put in jail for a drug charge—all these things bring shame to you and your family.

The same is true in serving God. You've got to know that you can't just dabble in this sin and that one and think you're hurting no one. Sin, especially gross sin, is so serious because you are dishonoring the one who shed His blood for you so sin would no longer own you. You've got to make up your mind to "go on" in Christ. Determine that you are going to grow in the Word, learn how to resist temptation, and live in a way that honors God.

Sad but true, even churches are full of people who can't seem to stop "sipping," "tipping," "dipping," and "shacking up." They say "Praise the Lord" one day, and go out and do what they want the next day. You cannot claim the cross of Christ for salvation if you refuse to live in holiness. The cross stands for the holiness that can be yours if you'll appropriate what Christ already did for you.

The cross was the greatest act of love ever exhibited. As Romans 5:7–8 says, "For scarcely for a righteous man will one die; yet perhaps for a good man someone would even dare to die. But God demonstrates His own love toward us, in that while we were still sinners, Christ died for us." Christ died for you and for me—even when we were unlovely, unlovable, depraved, degraded, and despised by others. Why would we ever want to say, "Okay, Jesus, you didn't suffer enough for me the first time you died on the cross. Get back up there and let me live like I want." The mere thought of it is abhorrent, and that's the stance you've got to keep.

Even if you have no fear of God and the judgment of His wrath, knowledge of Jesus' love for you and your corresponding love for Him ought to be enough to keep you from falling into sin. When your love for Him is strong and mature—when you "go on" with Him in your Christian walk—the idea of betraying Him and shaming Him becomes more and more unthinkable.

Let us go in! (Heb. 10:19–22, 26, 29 NLT)

Let's move on to the second thing. First, we learned that we have to go on in Christ. We have to learn the elementary doctrines of faith and mature in Christ. We have to be committed to honoring Him and living in holiness. Once we are doing all that, we have to do a second thing: we have to "go in." That's what verses 19 and 20 are talking about: "And so, dear brothers and sisters, we can boldly enter heaven's Most Holy Place because of the blood of Jesus. This is the new, life-giving way that Christ has opened up for us through the sacred curtain, by means of his death for us."

The new way of access to God that Christ obtained for us came through the curtain, or veil. When Christ's body was pierced, His skin represented the veil in the temple that covered the glory of God. When the nails, the sword, and the crown of thorns pierced His skin, a new and living way to God was opened, because now the "curtain" was torn.

By looking at the construction of the Jewish tabernacle, we can more easily understand this concept of going in. The tabernacle was composed of three parts. First, there was the outer court, which was visible to everyone. Here in the outer court were the laver and brazen altar. Then there was a veil that marked the entrance into the second part: the Holy Place. Here were the candlestick, altar of incense, and a table of showbread. In the Holy Place, the priest ministered every day. Then there was the Most Holy Place, separated from the rest of the tabernacle by a large, sacred veil. Once a year, the high priest walked into the Most Holy Place, and with the blood of bulls and goats, he made atonement for the sins of the entire nation.

The Power of the Cross

A lot of Christians don't understand that the cross represents access to the Most Holy Place. They live in the "outer court." They give a little shout at church on Sunday, and they might even get rambunctious and dance a step or two. At home they have one Bible verse on the refrigerator that they read each day (that's their time in the Word!), and prayer time consists of the ten seconds it takes to say a memorized prayer. Every now and then, they get really spiritual and up their prayer time to ten minutes in the car on the way to work or when running an errand.

That may be all well and good, and maybe it's better than nothing, but that keeps you in the outer court in your relationship with God. Living in the outer court might enable you to withstand about 10 percent of temptations. You'll have a little bit of victory here and there, but by and large, you're going to be rather anemic in your faith.

The Lord, however, is constantly calling us to go in a little bit further. And some people respond. Some Christians do move from the outer court to the Holy Place. They do more than pray on the run and read a verse or two. The Holy Place Christian will turn on some music and get alone with God for a time of worship. He loves the Lord and spends time praying and worshiping in the secret place. He's learned the joy of heartfelt worship.

Then there's the person who decides he's going to move through the outer court, into the Holy Place, and finally into the Most Holy Place. This place, as sanctioned in the Old Testament, was reserved for the intercessor, the high priest who went in once a year with the names of God's people over his heart and on his shoulders. In this most sacred place, he acted as mediator between God and the people.

The outer court is the place of fellowship, and the Holy Place is the place of worship, but the Most Holy Place is the place of intercession. It is entered only by those who know that the cross was the instrument that made this place accessible to them as children of God. In that Most Holy Place, the intercessor touches the face of God. There he can have communion with the Creator and enjoys the privilege of bringing requests before the throne of God.

As the place of intercession, the Most Holy Place is open to all who want it, and it imparts strength and fortitude to overcome every kind of temptation. Temptation comes to all of us, but how we deal with it varies. The outer court Christian is up and down, up and down in his spiritual life. Sometimes he feels good and is victorious over sin, and other times he feels bad and can't seem to withstand temptation. The Holy Place Christian has a little more victory, because he is at least a worshiper, but it is the Christian who regularly walks boldly into the Most Holy Place who is best able to defeat temptation. His eyes are on the cross of Christ, and he is not consumed with himself, but with the needs of a lost and dying world. He is an overcomer.

If we neglect to go in to the presence of God through the cross, we are in danger of trampling the Son of God and counting His blood as though it were nothing (Heb. 10:29). We've already talked about this in great detail, but it bears repeating. If we deliberately maintain a posture of sin, follow the world, and turn our back on the cross, we're trampling on Christ. That's what we're doing if we live careless, slipshod lives that excuse continual, habitual sin.

Let us go out! (Heb. 13:10–14 NLT)

The third secret of victory over temptation through the power of the cross is to realize that the cross enables us to completely turn our backs on the spirit of this world. Verse 11 of Hebrews 13 says, "Under the system of Jewish laws, the high priest brought the blood of animals into the Holy Place as a sacrifice for sin, but the bodies of the animals were burned outside the camp." Notice the last three words of that verse: *outside the camp*. That's where the sin offering was taken. Leviticus 4 describes the scenario of dragging this huge carcass of a bull to a site outside the camp. The sin offering was never burned in the camp—only outside the camp.

Now look at verse 12: "So also Jesus suffered and died outside the city gates in order to make his people holy by shedding his own blood." Where did the Savior die? Outside the city gates. If you recall the crucifixion story, you remember how Jesus was forced to carry His cross outside the city gates to Calvary's hill. Just like the sin offering of the Old Testament, the spotless Lamb of God was sacrificed outside the camp.

Verse 13 is the application of the two previous verses: "So *let us go out* to him outside the camp and bear the disgrace he bore" (emphasis added). Christ was crucified outside the gate of Jerusalem, and we must be willing to publicly identify with Him in the work of the cross. Each of us must make the decision of whether our permanent address is going to be in the city or outside of it. You're either going to be in the world, or you're going to be at the cross—you can't have it both ways.

Some of you are trying to do just that, keeping one foot in the world and one foot at the cross. You'll have nothing but confusion trying to live like that. It's like having two mailboxes; you will not get all your mail if you have two addresses. You've got to shut down one of your mailboxes so everything goes to only one address. Spiritually speaking, you're going to have to shut down your mailbox in the city of the world and tell the mailman, "Forward it all to the cross. I don't live in the city anymore. I live outside the camp, so forward it all to the cross!"

The Lord is issuing a challenge to you today. It's a day to choose. If you are serious about overcoming temptation, you're going to have to leave the world and all its enticements. You're going to have to step over the proverbial line in the sand and plant your feet squarely at the foot of the cross. You can't straddle the line; you can't walk in the world one day and the way of the cross the next. You've got to make a firm decision and then stick with it.

It's like the story of Lot in the Old Testament. Lot was Abraham's nephew, but he had a problem. When his and Abraham's herdsmen began arguing over grazing rights, Abraham graciously conceded to Lot the choice of where he wanted to live. Verse 12 of Genesis 13 records his choice: "Abram dwelt in the land of Canaan, and Lot dwelt in the cities of the plain and pitched his tent even as far as Sodom." Sodom was an extremely wicked city, yet Lot chose to link his fate with that evil place. He looked at the city, and it seemed exceedingly beautiful to him, so he chose it (vv. 10–11). There was something about that place that attracted him. His uncle gave him free rein to choose where he wanted to live, and he chose the city.

Maybe Lot didn't think his nearness to Sodom would affect him. Maybe he thought, "I'll just graze my livestock in the plains around the city, but I won't go into that wicked place. I'll be all right." But Genesis 19 shows us that was not the case. The Lord sent two angels to destroy Sodom, and when they arrived, who is sitting there in the gate of the city but Lot himself (v. 1)! Not only was he sitting there, but also he apparently had a home in the city, because he invited the two angels to go home with him (v. 2). Finally, in verse 8 when the men of the city wanted Lot to hand over the two men for their perverted wishes, Lot offered his daughters instead! So there's Lot's progression laid out for you. The closer he got to Sodom, the more carnal he became.

You can't play around with sin and think it won't hurt you. You can't live like the world six days a week and then think on Sunday you'll step over to the cross. You can't sing "Jesus, keep me near the cross," and on Monday morning head back over to the city. You'll be just like Lot, compromising more and more until finally you do something you never dreamed you would.

The world exerts a tremendous pull. You say, "It won't affect me. I can handle it." Before you know it, though, you're spending all your time there, doing what everybody else does and thinking nothing of it. You become more and more like the world and less and less like the Savior you claim to serve.

If you want to run after the world, sniffing and smelling it and taking a little taste of it, the devil will be only too happy to oblige you. You can make your address there if you want to, but as for me, I have moved my permanent address. I have left the world and moved under the shadow of the cross. That's where I live, and the Holy Spirit keeps me there. If I even start looking at the world, the Holy Spirit is quick to say, "Hey, what are you looking at? You don't live over there!" And I'm quick to answer, "Excuse me, Lord. You're right; I live at the cross."

That is how you avoid and conquer temptation. When you know that you're just passing through this world, that heaven is your true home, then you know that you're just a stranger here in this life. The things of the world have no pull on you because you don't belong to this world. You've got both feet firmly planted at the cross, and nothing can cause you to move.

Brothers and sisters, decide today to move your residence to the cross of Christ. Leave your former address and make a permanent move to Calvary. Throw away the key to the old house and walk in to the new one. In this house, you'll find freedom and victory from every bondage. In this house, you'll find room to forgive and heal any relationship. In this house are light and goodness that dispel the deepest despair and discouragement. In this house is such strength that no devil in hell can defeat you. In this house is the full power of the cross to deliver, heal, encourage, and uphold. In this house is Jesus!

OTHER BOOKS BY LARRY STOCKSTILL

25 LINES AROUND

THE CELL CHURCH

THE ONE YEAR DEVOTIONAL:
WALKING DAILY THROUGH THE BIBLE

CONQUERING IMPOSSIBILITIES

THE LAWS OF INCREASE

ER: EXTRAORDINARY RELATIONSHIPS

TAPE SERIES BY LARRY STOCKSTILL

THE POWER OF THE CROSS

ER: EXTRAORDINARY RELATIONSHIPS

THE LAWS OF INCREASE

CONQUERING IMPOSSIBILITIES

THE FOUR CUPS OF LOVE

WHAT THE BIBLE SAYS ABOUT . . .

PRAYER

COME HOME FAMILY CONFERENCE

For a complete listing of all resources offered by Bethany World Prayer Center, or to order any of Larry Stockstill's books or teaching series, call 225-771-1600, or visit their Web sites at www.bccn.com or www.bethany.com.

Printed in the United States
126946LV00002B/43-90/A